They came: they saw:
they created...

The Staithes Group of Artists 1894 -1909

Colin Bullamore

Cover picture,

'Lowestoft Herring Drifter'

Ernest Dade. Dated 1890

The Staithes Group of Artists 1894-1909

By Colin Bullamore

ISBN 978-0-9504109-5-1

Published by the author

Contents

PART ONE

DISCOVERING STAITHES

PART TWO

WHO WERE THE MEMBERS OF THE STAITHES GROUP?

PART THREE

INFORMATION FOR FURTHER STUDY

Part One

They came: they saw…

Discovering Staithes

Introduction

Why write another book on the Staithes Group of Artists?

On the surface this is a valid question as several excellent studies have been produced on the lives of specific leading artists such as Peter Frank's 'Sea Painter. The Life and Work of J.R. Bagshawe, 1870 – 1909' or the growing number of investigations into the life and work of Dame Laura Knight RA and her husband Harold Knight RA.

But when the Staithes Group is considered collectively, one becomes aware that there must have been a profitable interaction involving all the members. Each would have had a part to play in binding the group together. Around forty artists either lived in the area of Staithes, Roxby, Runswick and Hinderwell during the period 1894 – 1909 or regularly visited this area during the summer months. This was a considerable number for such a small fishing village.

Some artists such as Rowland Henry Hill, Mark Senior and Lionel Townsend Crawshaw even decided to continue living in this region of Yorkshire after the larger group had disbanded and dispersed around 1909.

It was partly as an attempt to consider the significance of each member that I decided to include in this study an investigation into the lives and work of some of the less well documented members and thereby present a more comprehensive assessment of this 'golden' period of artistic activity.

A difficulty soon became apparent in that whereas in the cases of many of the leaders of the group much evidence and data has been already published, in the case of several of the less well known little has been produced. Considering the fact that it is now over a hundred years since the breakup of the group, it is important to investigate any primary source information still extant.

A secondary and personal reason for undertaking this study is that for many years I have been impressed not only by the extensive amount of work produced during this relatively short period, nor the diversity of the styles or techniques employed by each member but by the constant high standard of achievement during this important avant-garde period in the history of British art.

I am sure that with the recent growing in recognition of the merit of the Staithes Group, more information will be discovered and they will then be ranked alongside the other art colonies at St. Ives, Newlyn and Lamora in Cornwall, Walderswick in Suffolk, the bases at Kirkcudbright and Cockburnspath frequented by 'The Glasgow Boys' and at Cullercoats near Tynemouth. The Staithes Group will be established as a major artistic centre from the advent of the 20th century.

Now, after a period of over a hundred years, we may not be able to fully capture the personal interaction that must have existed between the members of the group, nor appreciate how this isolated colony of artists in one of the most remote regions of Britain could be so influenced by the contemporary experiments of continental artists who were discovering new *en plein air* techniques which culminated in what we now call 'The Impressionist Movement'.

My main aim has been not to give a chronological resumé of lives of each artist, a birth, marriage and death account but rather to discover how a group of about forty individuals with such a varied range of personalities could so integrate and form such a coherent movement.

I wish to try and capture how their individual psyche can be seen in their oeuvre. For example, can one see in the sometimes heavy foreboding oils of Arthur Friedenson a glimpse into his periods of depression? Are the personal thoughts recorded in Laura Knight's autobiography '*Oil Paint and Grease Paint*' which she wrote about thirty years later, a window into her relationship with the people of Staithes? Can we capture her shared thoughts with Harold which eventually led to their need to escape the pressure of the intense life of the Staithes community with their constant hardship and fear and sorrow stemming from the frequent loss of lives at sea - a need which resulted in their moving to Cornwall to share the lighter atmosphere enjoyed by the members of the Newlyn School of Painters?

The period 1894 to 1909 became a chapter in so many artists' lives, a period which in most cases had a lasting effect upon the individual's future career. Can we look at the paintings they produced and relive the joy, the sorrow, the monotony of the lives of the fishing community yet capture their all-pervading comradeship?

The Staithes Group of Artists was there at the right time and captured a world which was to be for ever changed following the 1914-1918 Great War – a world which was so carefully captured by them that over a century later, we can still share in its being.

The uniqueness of Staithes

The older a town or village is the more likely it will have developed its own character and traditions and if this is coupled with geographic insolation as in the case of Staithes, those characteristics and traditions will be unique.

The protection given to Roxby Beck by the two nabs Cowbar to the west and Penny Nab to the east made the site of Staithes ideal for the development of a fishing community. This stretch of the coast is so exposed to onshore gales, yet being able to draw their fishing craft up Roxby Beck gave the community a much needed sanctuary. No other natural harbour exists from the River Esk at Whitby to the River Tees, a distance of over twenty miles.

Coupled with the natural danger of this Yorkshire coastline and frequent inclement weather, the fishermen of Staithes also experienced extreme hardship in the very nature of their work. Day after day they had to face the perils of the North Sea and year after year they became victims of the vagaries of the deep. In a gale in April 1815, twenty-nine local fishermen were drowned leaving sixteen widows and forty-eight children orphaned. In 1828 a further ten Staithes fishermen were drowned and another twenty-one children were left orphaned. There were many occasions when the members of the Staithes Group joined in the sorrow of the community when cobles with their crew failed to return home. It was this empathy with the Staithes people which resulted in such intense creations by the artists. Harold Knight's portrait of the grieving widow in her black mourning bonnet captures the depth of the women's pathos as she faces the emptiness of her future. This was perhaps the most moving painting from the whole of the Staithes Group..

It was the stoic nature of the Staithes people as a result of their environment which prompted Laura Knight to say in her 1936 first autobiography '*Oil Paint and Grease Paint*',

'An early winter morning, here comes a woman just back from the mussel-beds; she has been miles away over rocks at low tide, balanced on her head is about a hundred-weight, she walks with an easy stride as if carrying nothing. Her face is dark and stern – unapproachable – her carriage superb. She wears a tubful of bait for a crown.'

It was also this pressure of foreboding which eventually resulted in the Knights leaving the oppression they felt in Staithes for the Utopia they hoped to discover at Newlyn among the colony of artists working in that part of Cornwall.

Advent of the railway

and relief from centuries of isolation

It is difficult for us in the 21st century to appreciate the extent of the isolation experienced on the North East coast of Yorkshire even in the mid-19th century. Whitby which was so much larger than Staithes suffered from this isolation prior to the introduction of a horse drawn railway between Whitby and Pickering in 1836. Earlier attempts to construct a canal from Whitby to Pickering in the 18th century had failed and so until the introduction of a railway link, access to Whitby was either by the infrequent stage coaches from York and Scarborough or more often via sea using the sailing crafts which plied their North Sea routes.

This isolation was even more severe in the case of Staithes. Thomas Trattles, a local Staithes celebrity of some importance, had tried to persuade George Hudson, 'the Railway King' to include Staithes in his plans for the development of a rail system in North East Yorkshire but Trattles' plea failed as George Hudson excluded Staithes in the system. It was not until 1883 that Staithes was eventually connected by ten miles of railway to Whitby. This innovation resulted in the transmission of fresh fish three times a week to the larger neighbouring town but it also resulted in people being able to visit the picturesque fishing village of Staithes.

The last decade of the 19th century saw the beginning of an embryonic tourist trade between Whitby and Staithes not least due to what may be considered the quaint dress and customs of the local fishermen and their families. Centuries of development in isolation had been suddenly opened up to the rest of the world. Not only was the route along the coast via Sandsend and Kettleness one of the most attractive stretches of railway in the country but to see the vision of Staithes bonnets, fishermen working in their cobles and the whole ambience of a fishing community was well worth the effort of the day's expedition.

This facility of access was partly instrumental in the influx of photographers and artists and the eventual establishing of what became the Staithes Group of Artists in the late 1890's. Ironically the railway which was one of the manifestations of the Age of Industrialisation enabled these artists to escape from William Blake's *Dark Satanic Mills* to experience the unspoilt life found in Staithes.

Earlier 19th century art in Staithes

Although it could be said that the introduction of the Whitby to Saltburn railway in 1883 was responsible for the 'discovery' of Staithes as a Mecca for artists, it would be wrong to assume that this fishing village had not attracted earlier artists. Two leading painters from the mid-19th century who were prepared to undertake the demanding journey to Staithes by road and the sometimes perilous voyage if approached by sea were John Wilson Carmichael who travelled south from his base in Northumberland and Henry Barlow Carter who journeyed north from his home at 16, York Place, Scarborough where he lived from 1845 to 1862.

John Wilson Carmichael 1800-1868 was attracted by the similarity of the life style found in Staithes to that of the Northumberland fishing village of Cullercoates. As early as the 1820's he and other Northumberland artists had laid the foundation of what was to become the Cullercoats Colony, a school of artists which later became renowned for the paintings by the American Winslow Homer.

Carmichael like his precise contemporary H.B.Carter spent several years 'before the mast' which gave them both a detailed knowledge of shipping and its rigging and also the experience of the varying moods of the sea.

Henry Barlow Carter 1803-1867 is now becoming recognised as an exceptional water-colourist whose treatment of atmospheric effects and seascapes are most Turneresque in style. Although based in Scarborough, he travelled the Yorkshire coast from the chalk cliffs of Flamborough to as far north as Staithes and at times he even ventured up to the area of Bamburgh Castle in Northumberland.

A key element in his work was to capture movement whether it was to show the hazard of cobles trying to enter the safety of Roxby Beck at Staithes or facing the fury of the North Sea as they leave the protection of the stone piers at Whitby.

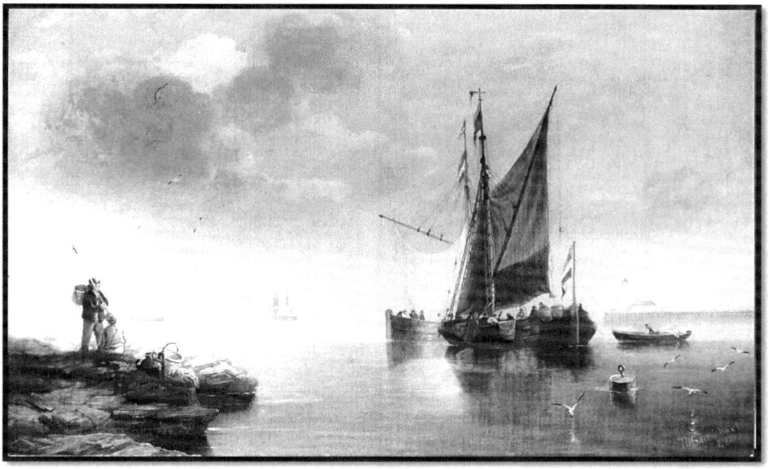

John Wilson Carmichael

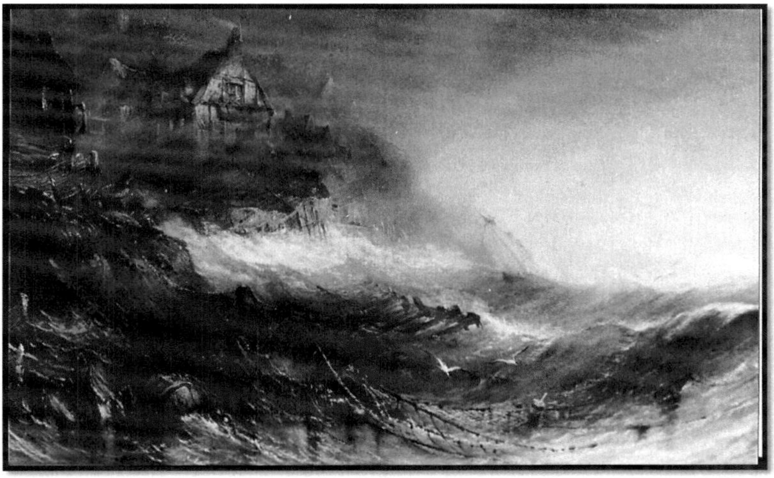

Henry Barlow Carter

Half a century separates Carter's treatment of cobles and other fishing craft from that of Harold Knight or Joseph Bagshawe, but one can see a continuity of style – a hazardous movement frozen in time. Although Carter preferred the medium of watercolour to capture the transience of the scene, the use of oils by the members of the Staithes Group produced a heavier texture which emphasised the pressure and dangerous element of the fishermen's task.

Carmichael and Carter had both 'discovered' the wealth of material to be found in Staithes and although they were only forerunners, their names should be always associated with the future artistic blossoming at the close of the 19th century.

Contemporary influence of photography

J.T.Ross and H.C.Morley

The fifteen year period of activity of the Staithes Group of Artists was also an important time in the development of photography in this region. Photography influenced art; art influenced photography. The result was a period of cross fertilisation with each medium benefitting from this association.

Also, just as the Staithes Group included artists with exceptional talent, so in the field of photography two men of exceptional ability stood out among the rest. These two were John Thomas Ross and Henry Charles Morley.

In several accounts of the Staithes Group of Artists it is claimed that it was Frank Meadow Sutcliffe who had the main influence upon the artists but in reality Sutcliffe's main sphere of activity was in the town of Whitby and in the villages which line the Esk Valley. Sutcliffe had great skill in composing a picture but unlike Ross and Morley, he often produced a contrived composition. Reality was often sacrificial for the sake of creating special effects.

Both Ross and Morley aimed to record rather than to create a view. In both cases they endeavoured to be a witness, a recorder rather than the designer of the scene and in this regard their aim was the same as that of the Staithes Group.

J.T.Ross, 1862 to 1929, was from a Whitby family. After serving for many years as a boiler maker in Turnbull's shipyard by the River Esk, he decided in about 1900 to move from being an amateur photographer to becoming a professional with his own studio in Whitby. He produced around a thousand photographic postcards which record in detail every aspect of life in this area at the beginning of the 20th century.

Strangely, Ross rarely worked south of Whitby in the region of Robin Hood's Bay but preferred to travel north and find his inspiration in the area of Runswick Bay and Staithes.

In this first photograph which he called *Fisher Girls Runswick* he has captured the young girls as they prepare to search for mussels to use as bait for the fishermen's long lines. Note that even at this young age, the girls are wearing their tradition Staithes bonnet. Ross has captured the need for all members of the family to help in the livelihood of fishing. Times were hard at the beginning of the 20th century and poverty was ever near.

One can imagine how this group of working girls would have appealed to Laura Knight who was often attracted to paint the children in Staithes. She records in her autobiography, *'In summer, my days were spent on the beach, rocks or quay: wherever children were playing I made innumerable colour notes and drawings. One day I executed thirteen small water-colours. My studio was littered with sketches of every kind of action a child would take.'*

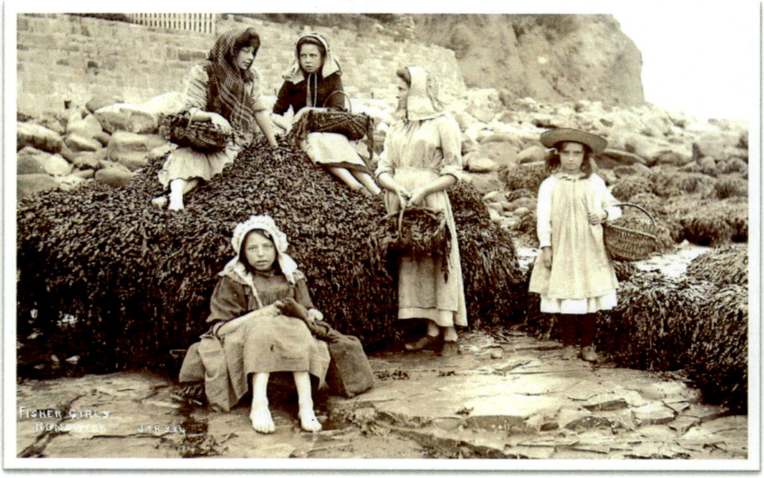

Fisher Girls Runswick J.T.Ross

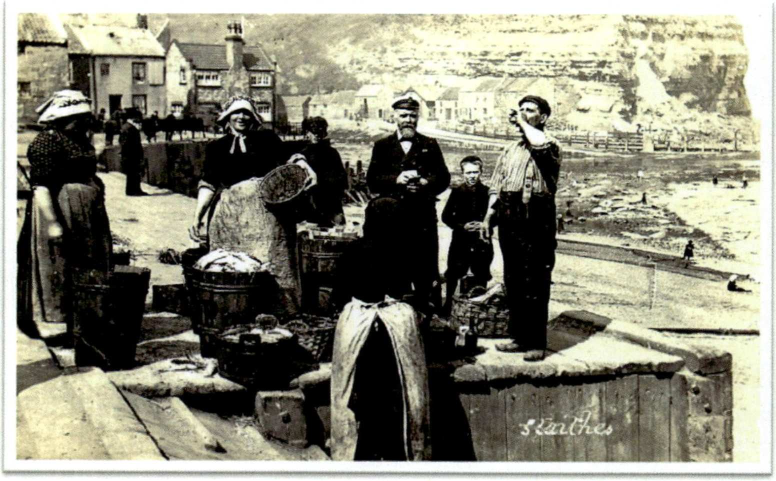

Staithes H.C.Morley

Henry Charles Morley was born in Nottingham in 1875 and like Harold and Laura Knight he eventually left Nottinghamshire to settle in Staithes. His move was sometime in 1903 for by 1904 and again in 1905 he had placed an advertisement in *Horne's Guide* describing himself as an artist and a photographer. His studio was established just off the High Street – the end house of Brown's Terrace.

By settling in Staithes, Morley was at an advantage. Ross, having set up his studio in Whitby, had to travel by train every time he wished to visit the Staithes area. Morley, on the other hand, was available to record any events in the village. He was able to focus his attention on a much more restricted area.

In the next group photograph taken against the background of Cowbar Nab, Morley has captured a moment of relaxation after the fish had been sorted and placed in wicker baskets. Like Ross' photograph of the *Fisher Girls*, Morley has shown how the fishing industry at Staithes involved the whole family. The wives are wearing their working bonnets and the heavy aprons protected their full length skirts. The central man wearing a naval cap has obviously made a note of the details of the sale. This is just one day in the life of the Staithes fishing community.

Unlike Frank Meadow Sutcliffe whose photographic plates have been preserved and reproduced in large quantities, both Ross and Morley's reputations have been hampered by the fact that their negative glass plates appear to have all been destroyed. It is only through the growing interest in deltiology (the collecting of postcards) that a picture can be drawn of the extent of their contribution to the development of photography.

Ross and Morley's world was in black and white. They couldn't capture the colours which Laura Knight describes so graphically in her autobiography. Yet within this black and white world, both Ross and Morley captured the environment and atmosphere of this small fishing village which so inspired the artists who were working there.

The birth of the Staithes Group

As early as 1868, a certain Indiana Trufitt had the bright idea that to promote her Staithes Hotel she should declare that Staithes was a favourite haunt of artists, with delightful good views. How near to the truth was her claim.

During the 1880's a small group of artists did start to centre their attention on Staithes led by William Gilbert Foster. By 1884 he was joined by Frederick Jackson and in about 1885 by Mark Senior and these three artists became the core of what was to flourish in the 1890's

The founding of the Staithes Art Club was in 1901 but before that date, several artists had already settled in the Staithes area including Hannah Hoyland (1890), Fred Mayor (1892), Henry Silkstone Hopwood (1900), John Spence Ingall (c1895), Earnest Dade (1889 though he was based in Scarborough) and Harold Knight and Laura Johnson (1897). So the stage was set for the 1901 official institution of the Staithes Art Club and what followed was the continued production of paintings which are now realised to be a major contribution to the development of British art.

Prior to 1901 the Staithes artists exhibited with the Yorkshire Union of Artists based in the West Riding but for the next five years they organised their own exhibitions, first in Staithes and then Whitby and it was not until 1906 that the group returned to the Y.U.A..

Staithes was still quite isolated in the 1880's and 90's, nevertheless, many members of the group had spent part of their training in academies in Paris, Antwerp, Bruges and Holland and so they knew that much of their work in Staithes was 'cutting edge'. The latest impressionist techniques were employed in conjunction with the artists' own individual development and style.

This study looks at these 'golden years' and at the lives of the artists who shared a common desire to create.

Continental influences

Just because the members of the Staithes Group chose to work and be inspired by the life centred around an isolated Yorkshire fishing village and just because their first priority was to capture *en plein air* the spirit of comradeship, the sharing of danger and sometimes the grief of death, nevertheless they fully realised the need to be au fait with all the avant-garde movements on the continent. And so in consequence many of them spent time at the Académie Julian in Paris to mix with the hundreds of students, many of whom would forge the history of art at the close of the 19th century.

Others like Harold and Laura Knight and Henry Silkstone Hopwood preferred to go to Amsterdam to study the masters of the Dutch School and then to work in the colony of artists in the village of Laren. A third destination was Belgium and especially the Académie Royale des Beaux-Arts in Antwerp which was visited by Arthur Friedenson in 1892.

It is hard to believe that such experimental techniques as Seuret and Pissarro's use of pointillism (composing the picture from hundreds of small brush strokes) was tried out in Staithes though it was found to be unsuitable for the Staithes subject matter.

The goal of the members of the Staithes Group was to use the most up to date techniques to capture the wealth of visual material they found in Yorkshire.

Académie Julian, Paris

The Académie Julian was established in 1868 by Rodolphe Julian (1839-1907) and although it included the traditional life classes, nevertheless it attracted many of the artists who were to change the course of the history of art towards the end of the 19th century.

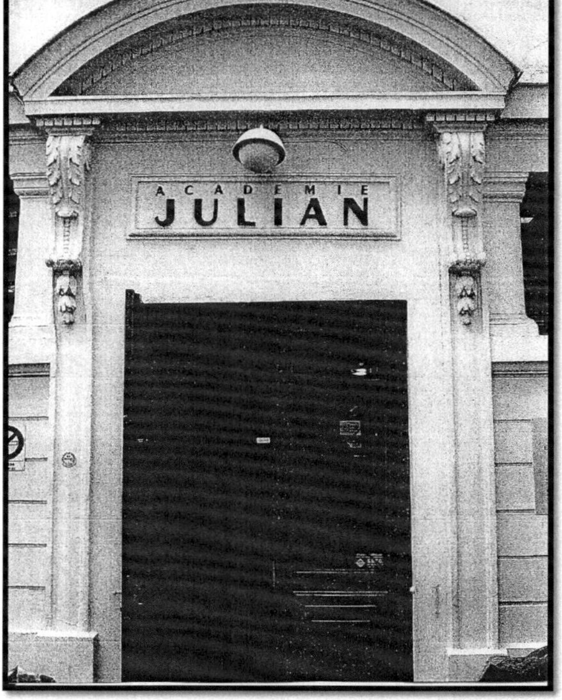

By the 1880's almost 600 students followed the training courses at one of the five branches of this progressive art school. 1875 to 1915 was the golden period of the académie which coincided with the period of Staithes Group of Artists.

The Académie Julian was particularly supported by American students who in turn influenced the development of art in the United States. In Europe many of the students were to gain recognition in the different art movements during this period including Henri Matisse, Jean Arp, Pierre Bonnard, Marcel Duchamp, John Lavery of the Glasgow School and Alfons Mucha.

It was through this channel that much of the avant-garde work in French art permeated back to Britain and although the Staithes artists were isolated, they were fully aware of all the developments on the continent.

Members of the Staithes Group who attended lessons at the Académie Julian include:-

Arthur Friedenson 1890 – 1892, 1896	Henry Silkstone Hopwood
Frederick Mayor	Ernest Higgins Rigg
Harold Knight	Isa Thompson
Ernest Dade 1884	Spence Ingall
Percy Morton Teasdale	Frederic William Jackson
Joseph Alfred Terry	

The Low Countries

The basic difference between the Parisian influence upon the members of the Staithes Group and that of the visits which were undertaken later to the Low Countries is that the attendance at the Académie Julian was part of the artists' initial training before they came to work in Staithes whereas the Dutch and Belgian visits were more a later quest for an update of the continuing art movements on the continent.

Robert Jobling had spent time in Holland for in the 1903 Annual Exhibition of the Staithes Art Group, he had submitted a painting called '*By the Zuydersee*' and the watercolour of Dordrecht which is illustrated later in the section on Jobling himself is also dated 1903. It had been previously thought that he, like Harold and Laura Knight and Henry Hopwood had visited Holland in 1904.

Laura Knight in her autobiography *'Oil paint and Grease Paint'* states that in 1903 the Knights arranged to go to Holland with Hopwood the following year. They headed first for Amsterdam to visit the Rijksmuseum to see the work of the great Dutch masters Vermeer, Rembrandt and Frans Hals.

Harold was influenced by the Dutch School especially Vermeer's use of incoming light to focus the viewer's eyes on the main subject of the painting. This is a technique Harold often adopted himself such as in the oil painting '*Breakfast*' which he exhibited at the Royal Academy the following year 1905. Here a small multi-paned window allows light to fall on the face of the man eating his breakfast while dramatically silhouetting the girl who is bringing him a cup and saucer. Rembrandt's various portraits also impressed Harold for he was already building up a reputation as a portrait painter and had received various commissions from around the country.

After studying the Dutch masterpieces in Amsterdam and looking to find a less expensive place in which to live, the Knights and Hopwood moved to the fishing village of Laren which had built an international reputation since 1880 as a centre for American, English and Dutch artists to work as a colony. Harold and Laura Knight returned to Laren at a later date.

As mentioned in the later section describing the 4th Annual Exhibition of the Staithes Art Club held in Whitby in August 1904, while the club was holding their exhibition in Whitby, the Knights and Hopwood had their own independent display of the Dutch paintings at Hopwood's own studio in Hinderwell.

Arthur Friedenson broke his studying at the Académie Julian in 1892 to spend some time at the Académie Royale des Beaux-Arts in Antwerp. Albert George Stevens also chose to study at the Académie in Antwerp whereas Joseph Richard Bagshawe trained under Van Hore in Bruges, another Belgian centre.

Annual Exhibitions 1901-1906

Several members of the Staithes Group were basically financially poor artists living amongst a very poor fishing community and so to generate an income to support their accommodation and food and to pay for the equipment and to reimburse the people who were prepared to sit patiently while they were being painted, it was necessary for them to sell the work they were creating. Commissions to paint portraits as in the case of Harold Knight or occasionally selling items which had been accepted by the Royal Academy may have given temporary relief to individual members but it was soon realised that an annual exhibition to sell their paintings was essential in any community of artists.

The First Annual Exhibition - 1901

The first exhibition was held in 1901 at the Fishermen's Institute in Staithes. Unfortunately it was not documented and the Whitby Gazette failed to make any reference to the event.

The fact that for many years no contemporary account of the first exhibition held in 1901 existed meant that we had to face the tantalising void in our knowledge of the Staithes Art Club. But the fortuitous discovery by James Hart in a public auction of the original diary of a certain Miss Enid Lucy Pearce Robinson who just happened to have been visiting Staithes during the month of August 1901 has meant that we can fill in the missing piece in this picture.

The diarist arrived in Staithes from Darlington on Wednesday the 7th August and stayed until Saturday the 31st of August which meant that she was able to visit the exhibition when it opened on Monday the 26th of August. She records how the stormy conditions on that day had affected the timing of the opening ceremony and possibly restricted the number of viewers. She also envisages an interesting scenario as to whether the exhibition was going to be officially opened by Joseph Richard Bagshawe's fiancée Miss Turnbull or possibly, by the Duchess of Kent!

This reference to Bagshawe is interesting as we know that later in 1904 he was instrumental in arranging the Fourth Annual Exhibition which was held in Anderson's Art Gallery in Skinner Street, Whitby. He was the secretary of the Art Club and so exhibition organiser may have been part of his mandate.

Enid Lucy Pearce Robinson appears to have been quite a gregarious person for she quickly developed relationships with the members of the art group. On her first day she records,

'I observed Mr Mayor and Mr. Friedenson on the Staith; they both looked hard at me. The Misses Jobling (all three) also came along and we bowed to them and they to us. I saw their father going down to paint over the Beck.

Mr. Bagshawe is engaged to be married in three weeks' time to a Miss Turnbull, the only daughter of a ship owner at Whitby and has been casting about for a house in Staithes, which should be to let unfurnished for the summer.'

She also recorded that –

Miss Thompson says that Mr. Rigg's dear old mother has been very ill and in consequence he has not been over in Staithes for some time now.'

And all this was recorded on her first day in Staithes. Obviously Enid knew the artists from a previous visit.

The Second Annual Exhibition - 1902

The 1901 exhibition must have been successful for on Saturday the 2nd August 1902, a second annual sale of paintings was held at the Fishermen's Institute. This time the event did not pass unrecorded and the following rather verbose report was given in the Whitby Gazette on Friday the 8th August. After a rather lyrical introduction the reporter gives details of each exhibitor with sufficient information of the paintings to enable us to identify them.

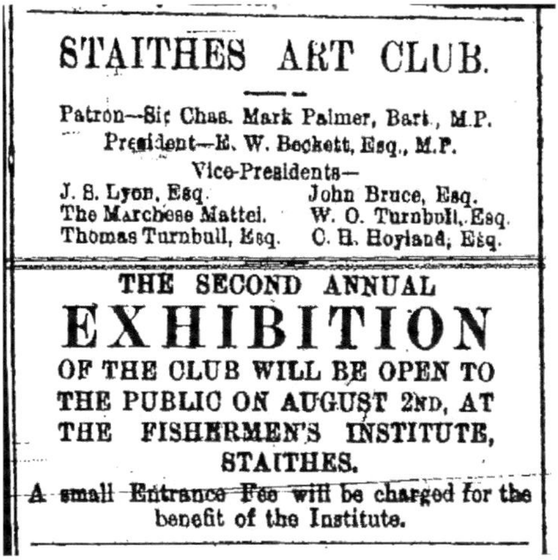

STAITHES ART CLUB.

Patron—Sir Chas. Mark Palmer, Bart., M.P.
President—E. W. Beckett, Esq., M.P.
Vice-Presidents—
J. S. Lyon, Esq. John Bruce, Esq.
The Marchese Mattei. W. O. Turnbull, Esq.
Thomas Turnbull, Esq. C. H. Hoyland, Esq.

THE SECOND ANNUAL
EXHIBITION
OF THE CLUB WILL BE OPEN TO THE PUBLIC ON AUGUST 2ND, AT THE FISHERMEN'S INSTITUTE, STAITHES.

A small Entrance Fee will be charged for the benefit of the Institute.

STAITHES ART CLUB

The private view of the second annual exhibition of works by members of this club was held on Friday, the 1st inst., in the Fishermen's Institute, Staithes. For many years now the district about Staithes, though more especially, at first, at Runswick and Hinderwell, has been the summer home of a few able and conscientious artists, who have discovered unconventional subjects for their brush, and, by careful study, have greatly improved their powers of perception, their appreciation of the relative values of lights and colours, and found alternative diversion between the rounded cheek of a nut-brown, sun-bonneted fisher maiden (we do not mean in its popular sense) and the rugged-faced son of Neptune who has spent a long life of unceasing toil on and by the waters of the treacherous North Sea. Like Whitby, the paintable bits about Staithes and Runswick are absolutely illimitable, and, winter or summer, it is all the same, artists may grew grey in the effort to characterise the people and places along this part of the north-east coast of England. And it is not too much to say that many of the cleverest of nature-artists have found inspiration hereabouts. With regards to the special function of which we write, there a gay and fashionable little assemblage present, which viewed with evident interest the representative collection of works on the walls of the upper room of the building which, from its large window looked upon the sea as from the deck of a steamer. Of large canvases, or pictures, there were none, save, perhaps, a fairly big picture of "Moonlight on the Bay" by C.H.Mackie, A.R.S,A., being a dreamy rendering of the bay of Runswick when bathed in the softened light of a summer moon. A picture which took our fancy most was a forcefully painted piece of shore work, with cobles in an angry surf, styled "Staithes Beach", by J.Richard Bagshawe, the colour and sentiment of which was thoroughly Staithian. "A Bit of Runswick" with the signature, F.W.Jackson, was, like all that artist's best work – rich in quality, and natural in colour. It, and a companion picture – upright – the second called, "The White Gate," are very pleasing pieces, and quite sustain the high standard of good work for which this artist is known among his confréres and the public. H.S.Hopwood, A.R.W.S. shows four little water-colours, a couple of which, "A Brother Brush", and, "Winter Quarters", give a fair idea of what he really can do with the thinner medium. "An Autumn Sunset", though from the hand of an unattached member, and a non-professional – Mr. Hirst Walker – appears with great credit among the other exhibits; indeed it is one of the most attractive on the walls. The same, however, cannot be said of his, "A Breezy Day", a touch or two of wrong colour in the sky, and a little too much local colour in the middle foreground militating against an otherwise good effect. "The Orchard", by Robert Jobling, is a very fine sunny picture, delightful in treatment, and interesting in subject – a young woman with a child in her arms, in an orchard, feeding some hens. A.A.Friedenson contributes three samples of his work, "Uplands" being a particularly pleasing piece: and Fred Mayor – famous for his pastel work – has four tender little subjects on show. Laura Johnson's figure subjects are cleverly painted, and add considerably to the general success of the exhibition. For a notable example of careful brushwork in oils, we can commend a couple of local bits by T.Barrett, of the Royal Society of Etchers. J.W.Booth does not do sufficient justice to himself in only sending "Haytime"; we should like to have seen something more of his excellent work. Harold Knight has four frames, of which we were particularly struck with

wilko

photo frame

"brighten up your space"

- silver effect frame creates an elegant look
- photos or pictures, your choice
- hang landscape or portrait

7 x 5"

(18 x 13cm)

"Launching Cobles", the colour being good, though the figures were a bit lacking in substance. J.Bowman and Isa Jobling complete the list of those who exhibit. There can be but one opinion among the fraternity of the brush as to the value of an exhibition of this kind, for comparison and criticism are the very soul of improvement, and are valuable guides to a complete success.

The Third Annual Exhibition -1903

Encouraged by the success of the second annual exhibition and also having more members of the group wishing to exhibit their work, the Staithes Art Club organised a third annual exhibition to be held in the Fishermen's Institute in Staithes. It was timed to coincide with the influx of visitors during the summer period. The third exhibition was duly opened on the 8th August and once again the Whitby Gazette gave a full report in the 21st of August edition of the newspaper.

STAITHES ART CLUB EXHIBITION

As stated last week, the third annual exhibition of work by the members of the Staithes Art Club was open in the Fishermen's Institute, Staithes on the 8th inst. There are, in all, forty-seven pictures hung on the walls, and a portfolio contains several other unmounted ones. It is not an easy matter to describe an exhibition of this sort, for it is difficult to estimate the real sentiments which artists themselves feel towards it. Do they regard it seriously, and as a fit and proper opportunity to display their best work? If so, then we cannot help but say that one artist at least is not adding to his powers, nor enhancing his reputation with the public. On the other hand, at least one other artist takes it seriously, and considers it his duty to hang his best and most careful efforts. This is apparent. Others seem to regard it variously, if one may judge from the pictures. There is no doubt at all about it being a thoroughly representative exhibition as far as methods and characteristics go; and herein lies its charm and value. Even the enquiring boy or girl who has never had a lesson in water-colour can *observe the method in painting adopted in the examples of that now famous water-colourist, H.S.Hopwood, by a study of the four sketches which are hung in the Seamen's Institute. They are all hastily painted – and show how they are done, a fact which must of itself denote inferior work. We know one of the most celebrated of water-colourist, who, when painting for a season from the then Mrs. Crosby's Hotel at Robin Hood's Bay, always locked his work up in a cupboard; and, if anyone approached him when working in the open, he closed his picture up. His greatest friends were not allowed to see his picture till finished. All the same they are an acquisition to the Club's show, these four pictures by Hopwood, for what there is in a name is there- and something more, for his "Study of a calf"' is like a bit of his own true self, it is full of strong good colour, and laid on with a sure and cunning hand. But a picture which combines correctness and forcefulness of drawing, quality in colour, and "experience" is F.W.Jackson's "Off to the rescue", which was sold on the day of the opening for £25. It is only of moderate size, but it tells its tale of modern sea heroism in truthful language. What else can one expect from such a clever draughtsman and colourist as F.W.Jackson who has shown annually, in England's premier picture place, some bit or other of the Runswick District for these teens of years? All the work of this artist is consistent, in that nothing is ever scamped but honestly endeavoured. Portrait painting may bring the dollars, but this- notwithstanding the temptations-does not succeed in alluring him from his true and only line-land and seascapes; and he flies away from his Manchester friends every now and then, to gain hope and inspiration on the shores of the Adriatic, or at his cottage by the North Sea.*

Of J. Richard Bagshawe's pictures at the Institute we are able to speak in almost unqualified praise. There is but one artist in every thousand who can draw that most difficult of all inanimate objects-a North Sea coast coble; but J.Richard Bagshawe is one of them, and we congratulate him upon the fact-though, all the same, in one of the pictures the stern of such a boat is not quite in true perspective. "Off Whitby Rock" is a fine, fresh, lilting piece of seascape, with its coble-crew lifting the crab-pots. "C'est magnifique" as the Frenchman would say; it takes you out on to the rolling sea, without, the possible discomforts of mal-de-mer. The only fault we have with it is the woolliness of the cliffs; they are right in colour, but not hard enough in drawing. "Wild Weather", and, "In the Dawn", are other examples from the brush of this conscientious student of the mystic sea.

A.A.Friendenson shows four frames, one-"A Showery Haytime"-being a very powerful painted scene on the cliff tops. Laura Knight is clever but fickle-and a bit tricky, too, sometimes as witness the lighting of a very attractive and beautiful work, "The "Road to the Farm". Her other pictures- of a decorative nature-are very engaging; and one cannot help admiring her great ability. Those who admire the bright, sunshiny picture, without much light and shade effect, will find something to revel in in R.Jobling's "By the Zuydersee" a charming bright creation. Hirst Walker, a very privileged amateur, responds to an invitation with "Hill-side near Harrogate". It is a small picture, but artistic in conception. J.Bowman shows three canvases, all of them delicate in tone and treatment. "Hinderwell Beck in June" by S.Gardner, is an admirable and satisfactory treatment of a green subject. A pair of small pictures including "Whitby Abbey from Sandsend" by Isa Jobling has had many admirers. T.Barret, A.R.E., exhibits half a dozen of his etchings. Other exhibits include J.W.Booth, Harold Knight, Rowland Hill and James Watson, (all of which show good work) and a pretty little pastel by Fred Mayor.

Though this report from the Whitby Gazette captures the writer's enthusiasm for the Staithes Art Club it is unfortunate that he spends so much time extolling the work of Hopwood and Jackson yet only allocates his final sentence to cover the paintings by J.W.Booth, Harold Knight, Rowland Hill, James Watson and Fred Mayor. What a missed opportunity in not giving us a more balanced account. He makes an interesting comment on a painting by Laura Knight saying that 'Laura Knight is clever but fickle-and a bit tricky, too, sometimes'. However his perception of J Richard Bagshawe's skill at capturing the complex line of the curvature of a North East coble must be commended.

The Fourth Annual Exhibition -1904

After holding three annual exhibitions at the Fishermen's Institute in Staithes, it was agreed that the 1904 event should be transferred to Whitby. There seem to have been several reasons for the move including the ever increasing number of paintings submitted - in1903 there had been 47 paintings on the walls of the Institute plus a portfolio of unframed works. The local fishing community did not have the means to buy the works and it was thought that the Whitby venue would draw a greater number of prospective buyers.

Joseph Bagshawe had the responsibility of finding a suitable gallery and arranging the necessary logistics for the event. The fact that the father of a member of the group, Edward Enoch Anderson had an art gallery in Skinner Street in Whitby made the choice much easier.

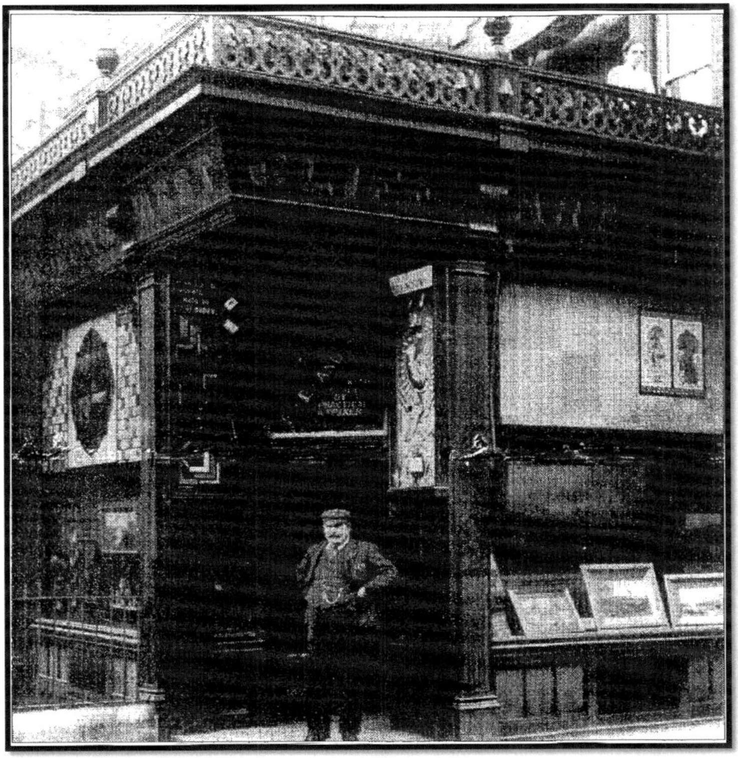

Anderson's art gallery in Skinner Street, Whitby

The Whitby Gazette once again fully reported the occasion giving the names of all 21 members who were represented.

STAITHES ART CLUB EXHIBITION.—This exhibition, which is being held on Mr. E. E. Anderson's premises, in Well Close Square, is the fourth promoted by the artistic colony which is associated with the picturesque fishing village indicated. The collection is varied, and of much more than local interest, although, of course, views of Whitby, and the adjoining coast and country, predominate. The number of pictures is eighty-six, exclusive of portfolio sketches, and the artists are:—Mrs. Harold Knight, and Messrs. Hirst Walker, Frank Mason, Rowland H. Hill, John Bowman, Isa Jobling, Harold Knight, James Booth, J. Richard Bagshawe, R.B.A.; F. W. Jackson, Chas. H. Mackie, A.R.S.A.; P. Morton Teasdale, T. W. Jackson, A. A. Friedenson, Owen Bowen, A.R.C.A.; F. Stuart Richardson, R.I.; Lionel T. Crawshaw, E. E. Anderson, R.B.A.; T. Wright, A.R.E.; Fred Mayor, and Spence Ingall. It is an exhibition of special merit; and affords an excellent opportunity for local art students to study some of the best work of the day, especially that of Mr. F. W. Jackson's. It seems mainly owing to Mr. J. R. Bagshawe's enterprise that the exhibition has, this year, enlarged its borders, by adding to the size and importance of the works shown; and we congratulate that energetic and able artist on the measure of success he has attained for the club's effort.

However, the move to Whitby had its problems, namely, that another exhibition of paintings was being held concurrently at the Lecture Hall in Silver Street which is next to Skinner Street. This exhibition was advertised in the Whitby Gazette as an '*Exhibition of Pictures by well-known Yorkshire Artists*' and included works by Stephen Frank Wasley and Frank Rousse, both highly respected Whitby artists and also at another venue there was a display of paintings by George Weatherill.

But most puzzling is the fact that at the same time as the Fourth Annual Exhibition was being held, Henry Silkstone Hopwood and Harold and Laura Knight had their own exhibition of paintings they had brought back from their stay at Laren in Holland.

This exhibition opened on Thursday the 25th August, 1904 and was open for several weeks at Hopwood's studio in Hinderwell near to the railway station.

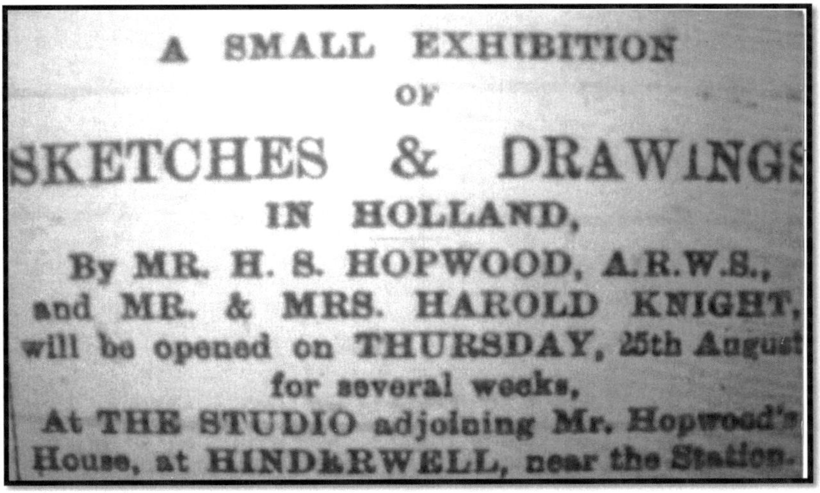
A SMALL EXHIBITION
OF
SKETCHES & DRAWINGS
IN HOLLAND,
By MR. H. S. HOPWOOD, A.R.W.S.,
and MR. & MRS. HAROLD KNIGHT,
will be opened on THURSDAY, 25th August
for several weeks,
At THE STUDIO adjoining Mr. Hopwood's
House, at HINDERWELL, near the Station.

Why would these three artists hold their own exhibition at the same time as the remainder of the group were holding theirs in Whitby? Harold and Laura Knight had entered paintings in both exhibitions but Hopwood appears not to have supported the Skinner Street display.

This is bound to cause us to ask the question as to whether there had been an element of difference of opinion over the move to Whitby. Or perhaps these three artists thought that work from Holland would not be suitable with the theme of the remaining group.

We just don't know what the reason was or whether the exhibition of Dutch paintings proved successful but it does illustrate an important factor regarding the Staithes Art Club. They were not so much an artist colony as found in Cornwall but more a loosely held fellowship with independence not only in the extent of their commitment to the group but also, and most importantly, they had a freedom to develop their own art as they thought fit. Support and encouragement from the members were the main factors which held the group together.

The Fifth Annual Exhibition - 1905

It has been generally assumed that the Staithes Art Club, after having held three annual exhibitions in the Fishermen's Institute, decided in 1904 to use the Anderson Art Gallery in Skinner Street in Whitby for future displays of their work.

Although this was the case for the 1904 exhibition, in 1905 there appears to have been a number of complications. In July 1905 Anderson the gallery proprietor established what he called The Rembrandt Gallery in Well Close Square, only a matter of yards from Skinner Street. It was his intention to have a permanent display of the work from a large number of artists from the area. In the Whitby Gazette for Friday the 4th August 1905 are full details of the artists to be represented. It is interesting that Frank Mason, a member of the Staithes Art Club, was included as was his own son Edward Enoch Anderson.

Anderson's new enterprise was duly reported in the Whitby Gazette on the 4th August with this special reference to Frank Mason. '*Another artist whose pictures are prominent at the gallery is Frank Mason. He is a faithful and vigorous portrayer of marine incidents and effects, and there are two or three very good examples of his style'*.

In addition to the opening of Anderson's Rembrandt Gallery there was also in the same copy of the Gazette notice of another exhibition in the Lecture Hall in Silver Street (off Skinner Street) of a '*Third Annual Exhibition of Oil, Watercolour drawings, etc. by well-known Yorkshire artists and others. Now open from 10 to 7'*.

STAITHES ART CLUB,

WATERLOO PLACE, FLOWERGATE.

FIFTH ANNUAL

EXHIBITION OF PICTURES.

OPEN THURSDAY, August 3rd.
PRIVATE VIEW - - August 2nd.
ADMISSION (including Catalogue), 6D.

So the Staithes Art Club decided to move to Waterloo Place in Flowergate and opened their exhibition on Thursday the 3rd August, 1905 with a private preview on the day before. Entrance fee was six pence, an increase on the former three pence and most importantly a catalogue was produced especially for the exhibition. This catalogue was used by the Whitby Gazette reporter as the basis for their review of the exhibition which was published on the 18th August.

STAITHES ART CLUB.

A Choice Exhibition.

The Staithes Art Club is to be congratulated on their fifth annual exhibition, which is being held at the Gallery, Waterloo Place, Flowergate. The Gallery being a small one, the pictures are necessarily not of the size of those exhibited last year, when there was more wall space at the Club's command. We think that, in this, the Club has been well advised in planning before the public works such as can be hung in any ordinary room, and of a quality that one rarely sees in modern galleries. The Club is composed of a number of artists who have, in a measure, settled in this district; but, unlike, many art institutions, there appears to be no particular leader, or style, such as was to be found in the Newlyn, or even the Glasgow school. The exhibition, in consequence, possesses a most varied and agreeable interest. Take, for instance, the works of Mr. Hopwood, Mr. Mackie, and Mr. Jackson, and, one might say, the majority of the members. Their aims are similar, but their methods are very dissimilar. They each try to give the broad truths of nature, ignoring almost entirely anything which would detract from the first impression

We will enumerate the works, in their catalogued order, which appealed to us as being deserving of attention. No. 1 is an oil picture by Mr. Teasdale, "The Cottager". Here we have a study of an old thatched house, in the foreground of which is well-known Runswick Fisherwoman, characteristically drawn and painted. In No. 3, Mr. Lionel Crawshaw gives us a bit of the holiday life in Whitby. No. 4 is "Etaples", by Mr. C.H.Mackie, a very Whistlerian impression of a well-known French fishing place. One would like to linger over this work, and study the drawing of the sand in the fore-ground, and the pools of water, which are certainly very masterly in their painting. In No. 9 Mr. Harold Knight exhibits an interior, treated much the same as his picture in this year's Royal Academy, which brought him into prominence. It is a beautiful presentment of old age. This is the best of Mr. Knight's contributions, and ought certainly to meet with a purchaser in Whitby. "The Bird-cage" by Mrs. Laura Knight, is full of daylight. It is a successful arrangement of whites and delicate pink Mr. Owen Bowen, in his "Winter Pastures" has seen his subject in a pictorial manner, if not altogether true in relationship; the sheep appear slightly warm, especially in the lights, which perhaps would partake somewhat of the cold blue of the sky. Mr. J. Bowman's picture, "Cutting Grass", is also a good composition. The scene is at Hinderwell. Mr. Bowman has well painted the sky. This picture, like the previous one, might possibly be improved by taking out a slight redness in the horses. There is a prevailing feeling here of hot weather. Perhaps Mr. Bowman has felt it necessary to force the reds so as to better convey this impression? In "A Sunny Morning", by Paul Paul, one can almost hear the crow of the cock and the cluckings of the hens. His picture is alive with the atmosphere of the farmyard. Look how well Mr.Paul has managed the shadow on the haystack. "Pasture", by Mr.F.W.Jackson, is similarly reminiscent of farm life. It is quite breezy. We feel sure the cows enjoy it. "Summer-time Staithes", by Mr. Robert Jobling, is a very pleasing figure picture, and, like the former works, brings us into the open air. The sea is moving, the atmosphere is clear, and the girl a pretty one. Mr. Hopwood has a strong painting of Durham. "Off Runswick", by Mr.J.R.Bagshawe, is a good example of his manner- free in treatment, and very effective in the suggested movement of the sea. "Red and Gold", to our mind, just misses being a fine work. Mr. Teasdale has not been so successful in his colour scheme as in the two other pictures of his. The red dress is overpowering. We omitted Mr. Friedenson's "Primrose Land" and "A Winter Eve" to group with Nos. 25 and 26, by the same artist. All these works are most ably painted, and are bright in colour. The handling of paint is not difficult to Mr.Friedenson; his career ought to be a successful one. We now arrive at a group of water-colours, and find Mr. Mackie at his best in "Whitby" (27), a drawing well seen, full of colour, and rich in every sense; as is also his "Stokesay Castle". Mr. Roland Hill's (30, 32 and 34) are all artistically treated. We should like to live with his "Old World garden", its lilies and roses. Mr.Hill has a good eye for colour. There are few drawings here that look truer to nature than this garden. No. 31, by Mrs.Laura Knight, deserves the centre of this wall. In all Mrs. Knight's works, one feels the human as well as the artistic instinct. Mr. Bagshawe and Mr.Knight are each seen in a broad manner on this wall. Nos. 39, 40, and 41 are by Mr.Paul Paul as also No. 47, which, we think, is the best of Mr. Paul's contributions to this exhibition. The painting is very reserved, and the cows are well modelled. Mr.Paul is to be congratulated on his entry into the Staithes Art Club. We are sure his inclusion is well merited. "Stirring the Pot", and "Beryl", ought each to be carefully seen. The last is a good portrait head. "In the Spring Time" is Mr.Jackson's principal contribution. It is placed in the centre of the wall. The hanging Committee evidently liked this picture, which is full of the uncertain glory of spring. Here we find the white blossom sloe, the golden gorse, and the running brook. In the "Little Knitter", we have one of Mr. Jackson's best figure pictures. The relationship of the tones has been carefully studied, and the painting done with apparent ease when we trouble to look for its technique. Mr.

J.W.Booth's contributions add much to the variety of the exhibition. Mr. Booth can paint horses. His three pictures, 42, 50, and 51 are all good examples. We especially like "Harvest". Mr. Hopwood takes us to a "Coffee House in Tunis", and gives us an impression of sunshine. As to No.53, by Laura Knight, we like "The Kiss"; it's so sweet. Mr. Jobling has wandered a little way down the coast to King's Lynn, and brought back a sunny and old-world-looking town hall. Mr. Jobling enjoyed painting the town hall, as also must Mr. Richardson when he painted 57 and 58, both excellent small pictures. Mr. Jackson's 59 and 65 are Whitby Scenes. The former found a purchaser on the opening day. We think the "Market Place" will also follow suit; it is so characteristic of the old spot on Saturday mornings. "Towing Out" is one of Mr.Bagshawe's principal works. It is quite a busy scene, contrasting greatly with Mr. Hopwood's quiet, cool "Passage in Tunis", a drawing grey, yet full of colour, as is also his "Tunis Bazaar". One would expect to meet with such a scene in Tunis – sunshine and colour in wondrous array. How well Mr. Hopwood has managed the reds in his drawing – just enough of it to enhance all the greys and prevent monotony. "Shipping Onions in Brittany" is an exquisite bit by Mr. Richardson. Here we have an old French port, suggested in apparently the easiest manner. Mr. Bagshawe's "In Whitby Roads" is seen at its best, it is a good and important contribution, to which the works of Mr.Ingall and Mrs. Jobling must be added to make up what we think is the best little show we have seen in Whitby. The Exhibition will remain open several weeks.

The anonymous reporter from the Whitby Gazette must be congratulated on a number of astute observations he made. He recognised a difference in the constitution of the Staithes Art Club and that of the Newlyn School and the 'Glasgow Boys' in that whereas in these schools a strong leadership existed in the form of Stanhope A. Forbes at Newlyn and James Guthrie in Glasgow. In the Staithes Group there was more a feeling of general independence. Members were at liberty to paint as they wished and use whatever techniques they preferred.

Secondly he recognised the impressionist element in their work when he commented '*they each try to give the broad truths of nature, ignoring almost entirely anything which would detract from the first impression*'.

Finally he appreciated the group's practice of painting *en plein air*. He describes "Summer-time, Staithes" by Mr. Robert Jobling, as '*a very pleasing, figure picture and brings us in the open air*'.

The Sixth Annual Exhibition - 1906

1906 was a momentous occasion for the Staithes Group. After exhibiting in the Fishermen's Institute in Staithes in 1901, 1902 and 1903, at Anderson's Art Gallery in Skinner Street 1904 and Waterloo Place in 1905, it was decided to return to the Yorkshire Union of Artists either because Waterloo Place was not a satisfactory venue or that exhibiting in a large West Riding city would result in a wider exposure to art collectors from the more industrialised region of Yorkshire.

Paintings from the Staithes Group of Artists were well represented in the Yorkshire Union of Artists annual exhibition which was held in Bradford from the 16th October 1906 to the 5th January 1907.

Fortunately the Union not only recorded which artists participated in the exhibition but also retained their addresses. This information is most useful in assessing the extent of the distribution of the artists in the Hinderwell, Runswick and Staithes area.

Several members of the Staithes Group had been regular exhibitors at the Yorkshire Union of Artists before they become involved with the Staithes Group, notably Rowland Henry Hill, Henry Silkstone Hopwood, Ernest Higgins Rigg and Owen Bowen but the information given here is only from their return to the Union in 1906.

ARTIST AND THEIR ADDRESS	DATE EXHIBITED
Joseph Richard Bagshawe	1906-09

The Old Rectory, Whitby	
James William Booth	1906-09
Haswell, Scalby, Scarborough	
John Bowman	1906-07
Sandsend, Whitby	
Lionel Townsend Crawshaw	1906-15
Blackburn's Yard, Whitby	
Charles Cutts Elmshirst	1894-1915
Elm House, Thorne, Doncaster	
Arthur Friedenson	1896-1915
Leandro Ramon Garrido	1906-08
Sleights, Whitby	
Rowland Henry Hill	1906-12
Ellerby Lodge, Runswick	
Henry Silkstone Hopwood	1906
The Croft, Hinderwell	
Montreuil-sur-Mer, Pas de Calais, France	1908-12
Spence Ingall	1896-1909
Banktop, Hinderwell	
Frederic William Jackson	1888-1915
Hinderwell	
Robert Jobling	1906
Dale House, Staithes	

Isa Jobling 1906

Dale House, Staithes

Harold Knight 1906

Staithes

Laura Knight 1906
Staithes

Charles H. Mackie 1906-09

Coltbridge Studio, Murrayfield, Edinburgh

Ernest Higgins Rigg 1906-15

Hinderwell

Albert George Stevens 1906

Mayfield Place, Whitby

Percy Morton Teasdale 1906-09

Studio, Cookridge Street, Leeds

Joseph Alfred Terry 1906-12

The Firs, Sleights, Whitby

****

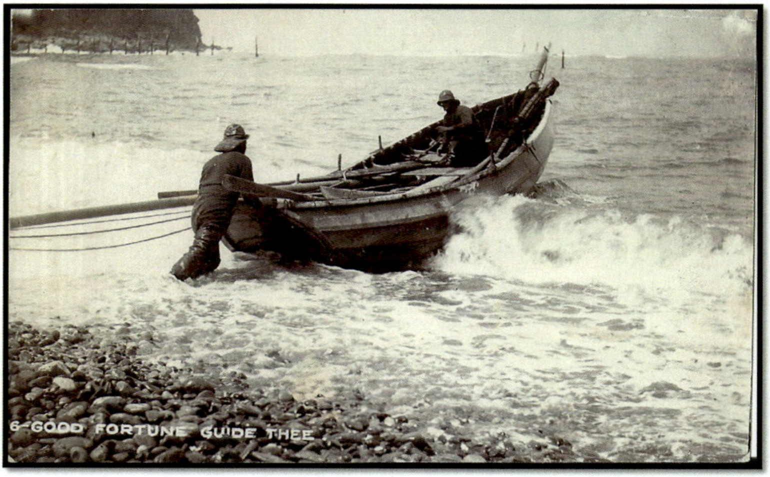

Postcard of Staithes fishermen launching their coble, c1910

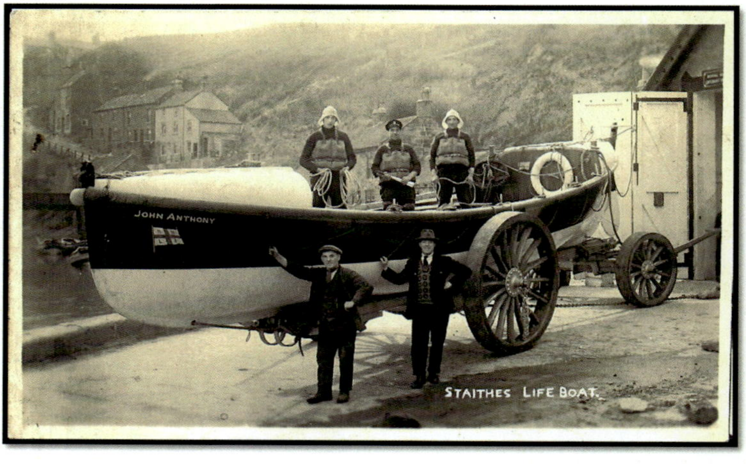

Staithes lifeboat c1910

Part two

They created…

Who were the members of the Staithes Group?

Founder members of the Staithes Group

It's said that mighty oaks grow from tiny acorns. The wonderful flowering of the Staithes Group from 1894 to 1909 had a small beginning instigated by three pioneer artists, William Gilbert Foster, Frederick William Jackson and Mark Senior. Yet though it was mainly due to their 'discovery' of Staithes and its potential for inspiring painting and though they may have attracted other artists to come and to share in their 'discovery', they did not assume a position of leadership as in the case of Stanhope Forbes or Alfred Munnings at Newlyn. Their enthusiasm for art and their love of Staithes was sufficient to attract artists from a wide area of the North of England. And so was formed an artist community with its own distinctive character, a fellowship in which each member benefitted from social intercourse and friendly encouragement.

This camaraderie had been well identified by Walter Sickert 1860-1942 when he said, *'It is well to remember that the language of paint like many others is kneaded and shaped by all the competitive workmen labouring at a given moment, that it is, with all its individual variations a common language, and not one of us would have been exactly what he is but for the influence and the experience of all the other competent workmen of that period.'*

William Gilbert Foster 1855-1906

William Gilbert Foster's name will always be associated with the Staithes Group of Artists because of the pioneer work he did prior to the 1894-1909 burst of creativity which he was able to witness in the last twelve years of his life.

He was born in Manchester on the 9th of May 1855. Although a capable artist he had only basic training from his father. He attended the Leeds Grammar School.

His association with Staithes started about 1880 with the two other precursors of the Staithes Group, Fred Jackson and Mark Senior.

He bought a cottage in Runswick Bay in the 1890's where he gave lessons in art. His most famous pupil was Owen Bowen who became a leading member of the group. The Fosters had four daughters and a son.

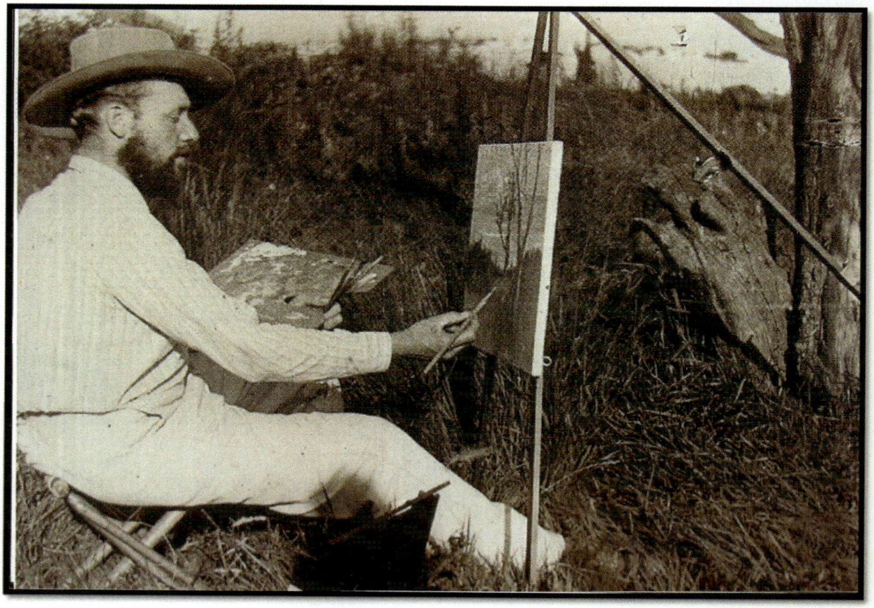

William Gilbert Foster painting en plein air

Like many later members of the Art Club, Foster exhibited nearly 40 paintings at the Royal Academy and was elected to the Royal Society of British Artists.

Foster's work is characterised by his attention to detail and, like the Glasgow Boys, he had pleasure in painting scenes of people working in their vegetable plots but in his case with a suitable background of his favourite coastline around Runswick. These characteristics are illustrated in this example of his work in the Pannett Art Gallery in Whitby.

Foster died in Halton Leeds on the 3rd of July 1906 aged 51, just three years before the Staithes Group of Artists finally disbanded.

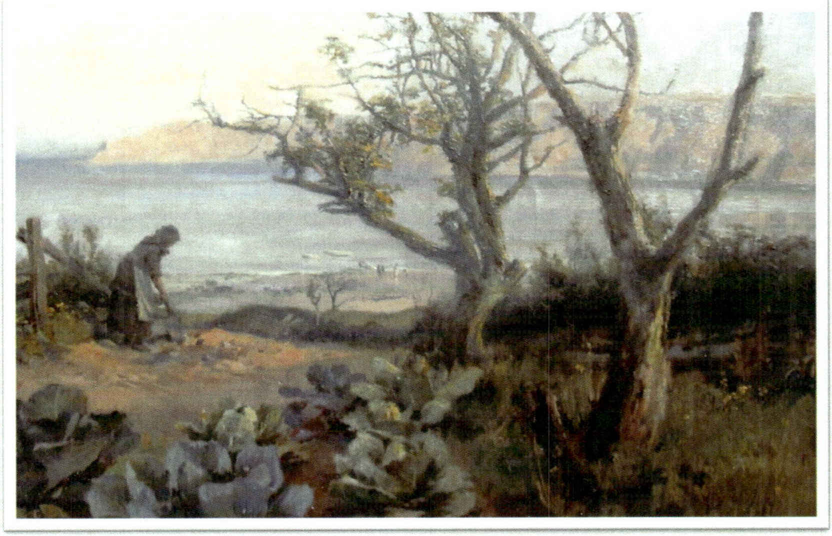

Courtesy of the Pannett Art Gallery, Whitby

Frederick William Jackson 1859-1918

Frederick William Jackson was born in Middleton near Manchester on the 23rd of August, 1859. His father was a pioneer photographer and also was an art dealer with premises in Police Street, Manchester and so Jackson was brought up in an artistic environment.

He trained at Oldham School of Art which was quite fortuitous for he came under the influence of William Stott RBA 1857-1900. Stott had himself trained in Paris and exhibited at the Paris Salon. He was associated with Whistler but the friendship broke up when Stott painted Whistler's Mistress Maud Frankin in the nude. Stott had an early death at the age of 44 while on a sea crossing to Ireland. A major retrospective exhibition of Stott's work was held in Oldham in December 2003 to April 2004 under the title '*A Comet Rushing to the Sun*'. Stott is acclaimed as an important British Impressionist painter and as such must have had considerable influence on the young Fred Jackson.

When the Oldham School of Art closed down, Jackson moved to Manchester School of Art and followed this in 1885 by studying at the Académie Julian in Paris under the tutorship of Lefebure and Boulanger. He exhibited at the Royal Academy from 1880 onwards and submitted works to the Paris Salon. In 1886 he was a founder member of the New English Art Club and in 1894 was elected to the Royal Society of British Arts.

Frederick Jackson's first visit to Staithes was in 1884 but after his period of studying in Paris he returned to settle by the Yorkshire coast, a region which he had begun to love. It was at this time that he met Anne Hodgson the daughter of a local farmer and after their marriage; they lived at Ivy Cottage in Hinderwell. Jackson soon built a studio at the cottage which in years to come became a meeting point for members of the Staithes Group.

Not only were the Jacksons noted for their hospitality and generosity but Frederick was always willing to help fellow members with their work. Laura Knight in particular received much constructive criticism as she strove to find a style of painting which satisfied her desire to be an individual, a style which would truly capture the life and environment in this Yorkshire fishing village. Years later when she wrote her first autobiography '*Oil Paint and Grease Paint*' she spoke with gratitude of the help she had received during those formative years in her career. Not only was Jackson a founder member of the Staithes Art Club at its inauguration in 1901 but his input and enthusiasm helped to mould the strength of this miscellaneous group of painters.

Jackson is remembered for his pursuit of *en plein air* painting in all kinds of weather. Laura Knight in her autobiography comments, '*He would paint out of doors in any weather. Under the mittens he wore his hands were swollen, stiff and chapped, as were the edges of his ears and the wings of his nostrils'.* Though he started painting in a very realistic manner, he gradually developed a distinctive impressionist style which was particularly evident in his later work.

Although he loved living at Hinderwell and remained there after the Staithes Group eventually broke up, nevertheless, he also loved to travel. In 1883 he had toured Italy with Charles Hodge Mackie and on later occasions he visited Holland, Tangier, Morocco and Russia. After Fred and Hannah Mayor had eloped to France, he stayed with them at their home in Montreuil-sur-Mer.

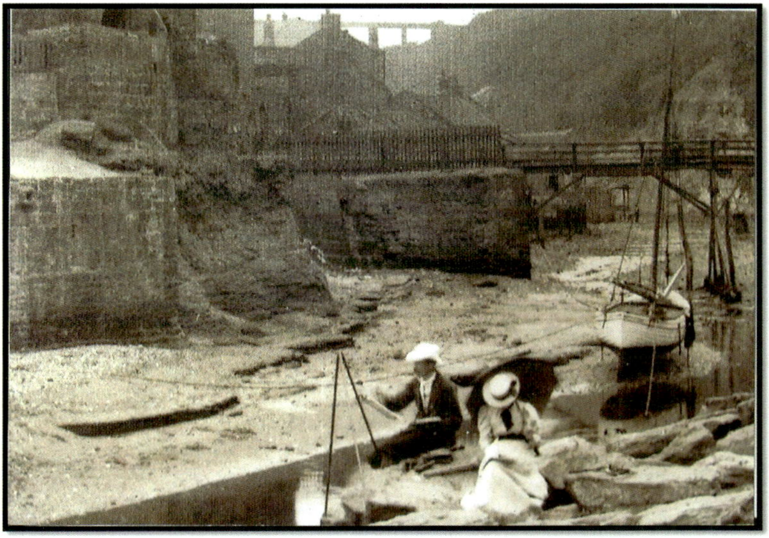

This photograph shows Laura Knight sitting beside Frederick Jackson as he paints a view looking down Roxby Beck towards the open sea.

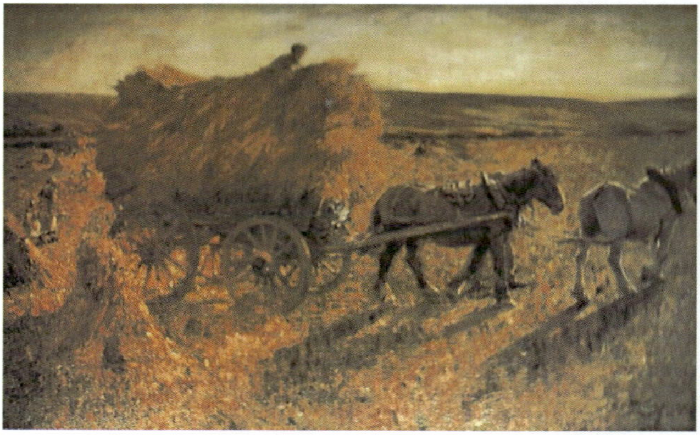

'Harvest Time' Frederick William Jackson. Courtesy of the Pannett Art Gallery

Frederick Jackson died in Middleton on the 25th of February, 1918 in his 59th year.'

Mark Senior 1862-1927

Mark Senior, the third of the trinity of founder members of the Staithes Group was born at Hanging Heaton near to Dewsbury on the 16th of March, 1862. His artistic training commenced in 1880 when he enrolled as a student at the Wakefield School of Art.

His first exhibit at the Royal Academy in 1892 titled '*Evening*' was the beginning of his regular submission of works until 1924.

The titles of his paintings over the nineteen years of association with the Royal Academy illustrate the width of the subject matter Senior painted. Naturally the Yorkshire coast is represented with 1896 *'Pastures by the Sea'*, 1899 *'Preparing to Bait'*, 1911 *'Away to the Sea* 'and 1916 *'The Beach'*. It is not surprising that in 1907 after his visit to Belgium the work was *'A Flemish Fishmarket'*.

The effect of light and shadow is found in the paintings of 1900 *'Nightfall'*, and 1909 *'Spring Sunlight'*,

But what is interesting is that from 1909 the word 'Spring' is often found in the description with 1909 *'Spring Sunlight'*, 1910 *'Spring'*, 1911 *'Springtime'*, 1917 *'A Spring Morning'*, and 1918, 1919 and 1924 just simply *'Spring'*. Perhaps there was some psychological reason for the concept of spring being so predominant in his work or simply the fresh colours found at springtime had a special appeal to him.

Mark Senior's paintings, if they had to be classified, were post-impressionist. This phrase was coined in 1910 by the critic Roger Fry to describe the extension of impressionism with an intensity of colour, with a thicker application of paint and this tendency is very evident especially in Mark Senior's oil paintings.

He was fully au fait with the latest developments on the continent and had close relationships with many of the leading British artists of the time. In 1906 he visited Philip Wilson Steer at Walderswick in Suffolk which, like Staithes, was a centre for a contemporary artist colony. Other friends included Frank Brangwyn, James McNeill Whistler and William Orpen.

Perhaps the most fruitful association Mark Senior had was with the affluent West Riding philanthropist Sam Wilson. Wilson, upon his death, bequeathed his entire personal collection of modern British art to the City of Leeds Art Gallery. Senior, for ever developing contacts, was responsible for arranging introductions which were beneficial to Sam Wilson in his pursuit of works of art. The prime example was the commission Senior's friend Alfred Gilbert had from Sam Wilson to design a monumental chimney piece especially for the Art Gallery in Leeds. Sam Wilson's collection is now housed in a new wing of the art gallery.

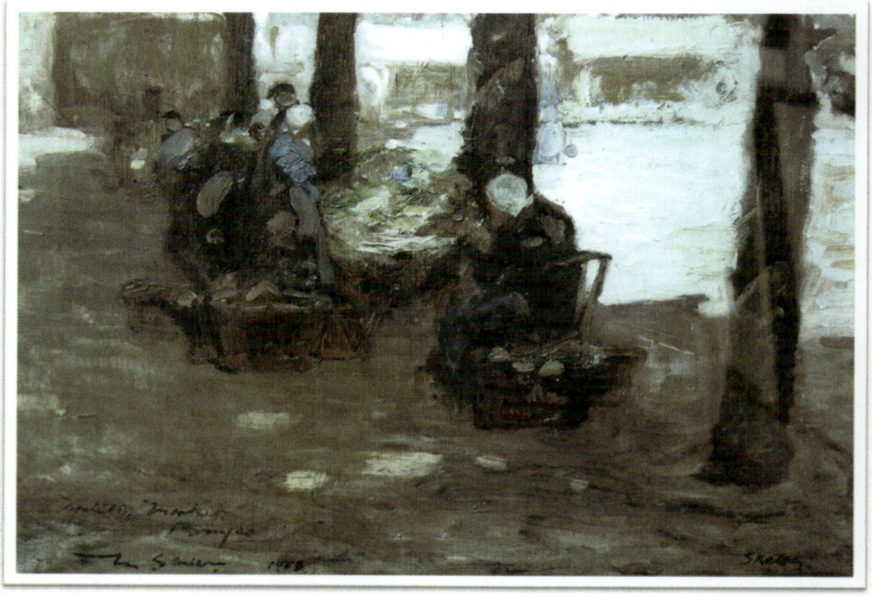

'A Market in Bruges' Mark Senior. Courtesy of the Pannett Art Gallery

Mark Senior had a special attraction to the medieval city of Bruges in northern Belgium Its network of waterways and many bridges made it the 'Venice of the North'. He visited the Flanders area several times between 1907 and 1910. The 1908 visit was with Miss Florence Hess (1891-1974) who had been his pupil since 1905 and with Gertrude Hudson. (Gertrude Hudson sold land at RunswickBay to Mark Senior so that he could build his house Hillside.) In 1910 he visited Albert Gilbert's Bruges home. Albert Gilbert RA, who is remembered today for having designed the Eros Monument in Piccadilly Circus, was a great friend of Mark Senior and they helped each other in finding clients for their work.

Later in life Mark Senior became dissatisfied with his early work and actively bought it back to destroy it. This was not dissimilar to Laura Knight who destroyed much of her early Staithes work. Both artists did not want to be judged by their early, and perhaps in their opinion, sometimes immature paintings and drawings.

Mark Senior, like Rowland Hill, Fred Jackson and Albert Stevens was one of the few members of the Staithes Group who decided to remain in this region of Yorkshire after the main group broke up in 1909.

He died on the 1st of January, 1927 at Hillside in Runswick Bay aged 54 and he was buried at St. Hilda's Parish Church in Hinderwell in that part of the country he loved so much.

Women artists in the Staithes Group

It is not surprising to find a correlation between the general striving of women for some degree of equality during the last decade of the 19th century, a striving centred upon the Suffragette movement for political franchise and the strength of character of the three women members of the Staithes Group. Art was a medium in which they were able to express their emotions and their views on society just as forcefully as any male member of the group.

The Académie Julian in Paris had been foremost for many years in giving women students an equal opportunity to develop their talent even though they were often banned from live classes. This is a women's class at the Académie Julian in the late 19th century.

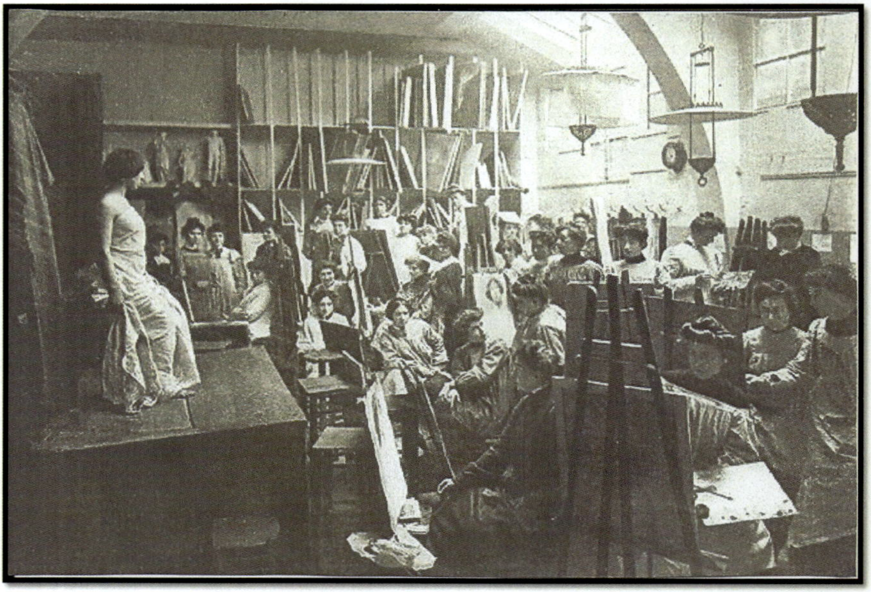

All three women in the Staithes Group became married during their time at Staithes and it is interesting to notice a change in their work after their marriage. Laura Knight, who was married to Harold in 1903 when she was 26 years old, continued to discover her artistic identity and to dedicate all her energy to achieving her goal of being an independent artist as able as the men within the group.

In the case of Isa Thompson, the strength and confidence she displayed during her time at Cullercoats and the early years at Staithes before she married Robert Jobling seemed to change as she turned more to painting garden scenes and flowers which had been traditionally the domaine of so many amatuer women artists in the 19th century.

Hannah Mayor, who was married to Fred Mayor in 1902, also seemed to change towards producing still life images of vases of flowers especially after her husband died in 1916 at the tragically young age of 49.

It would be interesting to assess the interaction between these three women during their time with the Staithes Group but what ought to have been our main source of information, the two autobiographies written by Laura Knight, contain hardly any reference to the two other women.

Many suggestions have been made as to why Laura appears to ignore Isa and Hannah but perhaps it is best just to say that they had no part to play in her own development and therefore didn't receive any mention.

However, it is a little ironic that Laura Knight displays such affection towards Henry Hopwood's wife. Harold and she had been '*taken in hand*' by Mrs. Hopwood who provided them with '*food, warmth and good conversation*' and especially appreciated by Laura, she was provided with '*one or two up-to-date clothes.*' A similar affection was shown by Laura towards the wife of Fred Jackson.

After having discussed the work of the founders of the group, Gilbert Foster, Frederick Jackson and Mark Senior, I've chosen to consider firstly the women in the group not as a gesture of ladies first but simply becasuse both Isa and Hannah were associated with the group from the very beginning and were accepted as full members as early as 1901.

Isabella (Isa) Jobling (née Thompson) 1851-1926

From Cullercoates to Staithes

Isa Thompson was born in Newcastle in 1851. After studying in Paris she settled in Cullercoates and joined the well established artist colony. There existed a close similarity between Cullercoates and Staithes both in the dress of the fisherwives, the method of fishing and also the use of the traditional north east fishing vessel, the coble. Isa appears to have worked in Cullercoates as an independent artist during the 1880's which was in itself a remarkable thing to do in those days.

She submitted work into the 1883 Gateshead Fine Art and Industrial Exhibition.

It was also while living in Cullercoates that she first met the artist Robert Jobling and his wife Annie Chamber and their four children. Years later in 1893, while they were both working in Staithes, Robert was to marry Isa after the death of his first wife. Early examples of Isa's work during her Cullercoates period are to found in the Laing Art Gallery in Newcastle.

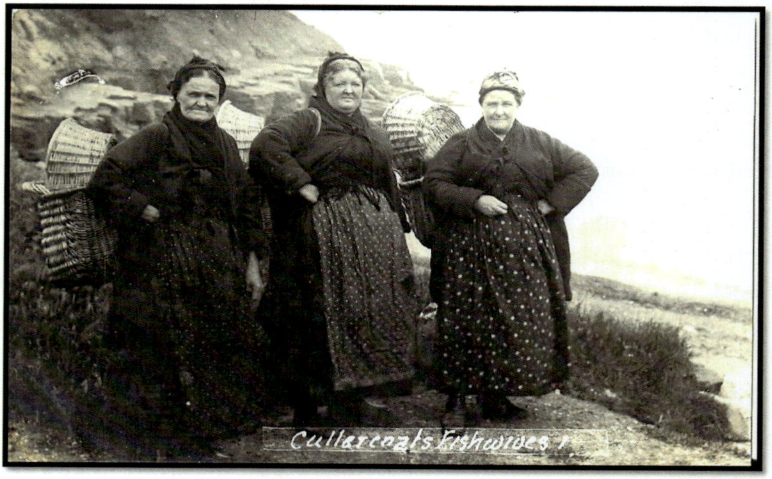

It appears that Isa visted Staithes in 1889 and after deciding to settle there, she became a founder member of the Staithes Art Club in 1901. She already had been exposed to the demands of living in a fishing community and had produced many strong canvases capturing the hardship of the fishermen's labours and so she was able to enter the Staithes Group with a well developed style. She was, in fact, as good as the male members and exhibited regularly in the Annual Exhibitions from 1901 until the group returned to the Yorkshie Union of Artists in 1906. Isa was a regular exhibitor in Newcastle at the Laing Art Gallery and the Bewick Club and nationally at the Royal Society of Arts, the

Royal Academy, the Royal Scottish Academy and at galleries in Birmingham, Glasgow, Liverpool and Manchester.

It is unfortunate that after marrying Robert Jobling her style somewhat changed with more interest being shown in capturing garden scenes and flowers. But when we consider the strength of her works from Cullercoates and the early years in Staithes, she must stand as a major contributor to the work of the Staithes Group of Artists..

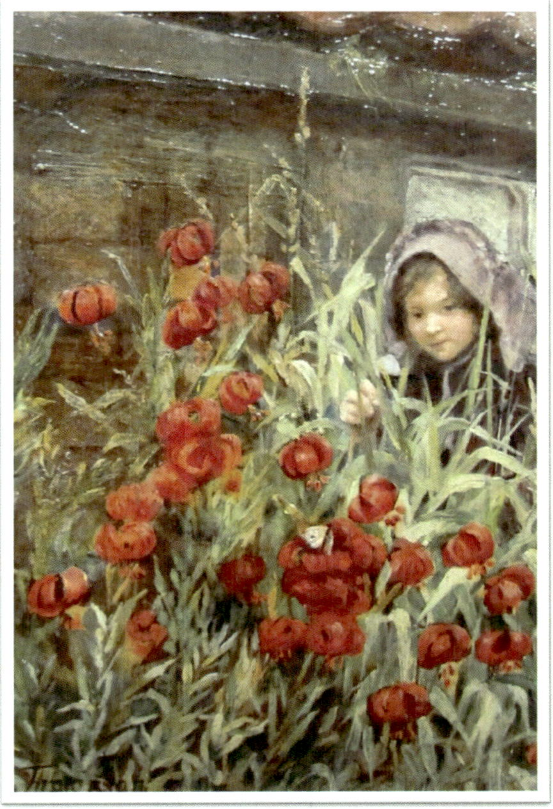

This is a typical later work of Isa Jobling. Coutesy of the Pannet Art Gallery

Laura Knight (née Johnson) 1877-1970

Staithes revisited

In Laura Knight's 1936 autobiography *'Oil Paint and Grease Paint'* one senses that she is speaking to us personally as she recalls the time she made Staithes her home.

It could be said that she discovered herself during the early and formative years she spent in Staithes. Not only was she influenced by the other members of the artist community but she immediately discovered an affinity with the area and with the local Staithes people. To quote her own words –

It was there (Staithes) *that I found myself and what I might do. I loved it passionately, overwhelmingly. I loved the cold and the northerly storms when no covering would protect you. I loved the strange race of people who lived there, whose stern almost forbidding exterior formed such contrast to the warmth and richness of their nature.*

This euphoria lasted for several years, punctuated only by Harold and Laura's three visits to Holland but by 1907 it had become obvious to them that they ought to search for a more temperate clime and so they started to consider moving further south. Despite their love for Staithes, they eventually moved to join the well-established school of artists in Newlyn in Cornwall. But Laura's love for Staithes and the people she had grown to love still continued. In this letter to a Mrs. Langster and dated the 26th May, 1967, sixty years after leaving the Yorkshire village, Laura Knight testified to her love for the Staithes area.

Dear Mrs. Langster,

Please forgive my delay in answering your delightful letter. To write the name Langster takes me back straight to Staithes, the memory of which is so beautiful in every way. Perhaps the happiest days of my life were spent with the dear friends I made there... great, good and wonderful people. They are all dear to my heart today.

I wish I could have said something about Staithes in my B.B.C. broadcast but as you say 'one cannot put a life time into a few minutes' and you are more or less told what you must talk about.

All the same if I ever get the chance to tell of the love, help and sympathy I knew in Staithes I shall bless the opportunity.

You say you are not a good hand at writing a letter. I think yours was a beautiful letter which moved me very much. How wonderful it is that your husband remembers me. I well remember painting Sarah Jane and 'Dimples'.

With love to all my dear friends,

Affectionately yours

Laura Knight

Laura Knight's frequent use of the first person singular in her first autobiography has resulted in one having the experience of actually sharing in the events of her years in Staithes, although of the forty-five chapters, only seven cover this early period.

It is unusual for a person to leave a record of their lives in two different media but Laura Knight is exceptional in that her written account supplements the visual record she left in her paintings.

It is a little surprising to find that her autobiography is inclined to be rather self-centred. Harold, who shared so much of her life, receives only a passing reference in these early chapters and except for Fred Mayor, she gives little information regarding the interaction between the different members of the Staithes Group.

However, within these seven Staithes chapters we do find many clues as to her process of maturing artistically and discovering herself through her art. By the time Harold and Laura left Staithes to join the Newlyn Group she had gained that confidence which she was to display throughout her life.

It is surprising how such a comment as '*the drawing of hands and arms held for me a special interest; I studied their movement every chance I had. Sketch-books were filled with nothing else.*' actually opens up a window into an important aspect of her artistic objectives. This reference to the treatment of the sitter's hands I found very relevant in the 2013 exhibition at the National Portrait Gallery in London '*Laura Knight Portraits*'. Yes, one is impressed by the detail of the facial expression or the glint of light in the eyes yet in each portrait the artist showed skill in the masterly painting of the hands. So often throughout the history of portraiture, the presentation of the hands fails to reach the quality of the facial treatment.

But with Laura Knight this is not the case. The hands are just as important in capturing the nature of the sitter as any intense concentration on the face. Take for example her 1943 painting of '*Ruby Loftus Screwing a Breech Ring*'. She has captured the way that Ruby's hands emphasize the cold contour of the lathe on which she is working. The machine and Ruby are as one unit. Each is dependent upon the other. Even the finger nails reflect the light from the spot light which gives the painting a focal point.

On the other hand in the 1930 painting '*Ballet Girl and Dressmaker*' the artist shows that the dancer's hands are lightly resting upon her crossed legs while in contrast she has captured the contortion of the dressmaker's hands as she manipulates the pair of scissors.

Another aspect of the artist's skill is the use of a simple line to capture the relationship between the individual fingers on the hand. In this 1926 etching the hand position of the central girl endorses the gesture of her face. The hand and face is one unit and captures the apparent puzzlement experienced by the girl. On the other hand the third girl on the right has her hand crossed on her knee and thereby shows an element of control. The artist has not recorded the position of the hands of the girl on the left but the facial expression shows that she is in the process of summing up the thoughts of the other two. How successful was Laura Knight by using such a simple treatment to capture such contrasting feelings and thoughts.

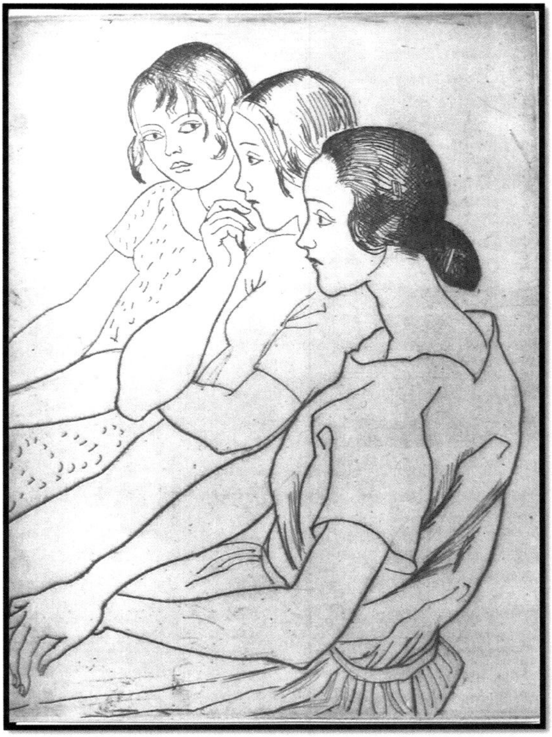

Although the portraits from the Staithes period are often characterised by the use of a rather heavy palette and the contours of the hands may not be as well defined as in the paintings she produced during the later Newlyn period or her time with gypsies, the circus or even as a war artist, nevertheless, even at this early stage in her development Laura Knight uses the hands to centre the viewer's attention on the activity of the sitter. In the sensitive treatment of '*Girl playing with a cat*' from about 1903, or '*The Knitting Lesson*' where a mother guides the young girl's hands in performing the next stitch and the two portraits from about 1900 of a woman '*Peeling Potatoes*' and

'Plucking the Goose', the theme of each painting is centred upon the treatment of the sitter's hands.

Colour meant everything to Laura Knight. Throughout her autobiography, whenever she recorded an incident from her time in Staithes, even after a period of thirty years, her thoughts were dominated by the recollection of the colours which she had committed to memory. In this brief extract from her autobiography which describes the changing light during an evening in Staithes, I have underlined all references to colour to illustrate the extent of her mental palette.

Now is a summer evening: the sun is down behind the hills, deep-toned and sharp against the gold of the sky; shadow lies over village quay and beach.. A man is half-hidden under a heap of purple blackish nets; another balances oars on his shoulders; a boy carries a string of coloured bladders used to buoy up the nets.

During the herring season, one often sees such a scene, darkly rich against the sea, turquoise splashed with indigo in the last rays of the sun.

The sun gilds the brightly painted cobles in the Wyke. One boat disappears round the Penny Nab, her red-tanned mainsail, mizzen and jibs all set. In another boat a man hauls the sails Venetian red drapery unfolds. A big main sail goes up, a patch of shining white that has not yet seen the barking copper. The women's knitting needles click as they stand gossiping on the quay, their figures in sombre black and lavender silhouette.

A question often asked is why in view of the fact that Laura Knight worked in Staithes for so many years and that her working days could be all the hours of daylight, are there relatively so few examples of her Staithes output in national art galleries or even that come onto the open market? It is her post-1907 work, centred upon her time at Newlyn, or the years spent recording circus life, theatre, gypsies or as a war artist that her reputation is mainly based.

The reason for this is rather complex. From entering the Nottingham School of Art at the young age of thirteen, she was aware not only of her own innate ability to draw but also the need to learn how to develop the skills required to become an artist. Even during her time at the Nottingham School of Art she would try to copy the technique of Harold Knight who was an accomplished senior student. Later at Staithes she was prompted by Charles Mackie to learn to 'do her own thing', to capture the view as she saw it.

This development required her to undertake countless attempts and a corresponding number of what she classed as failures. She was so self-critical with the results that much of what she produced at Staithes she later destroyed.

Sometimes she destroyed her work following a series of disappointments. Her first big picture which she called *'Off the Herring Fishing'* was sent three times to the Academy and each time it was rejected. As she records in her autobiography *'Finally I cut it up to make a roaring fire in my studio stove'*.

Another reason for her destroying her work was the logistics of visiting the group of artists in Laren in Holland. She could not transport all her work and so what she considered of insufficient merit, she destroyed.

An important part of her personality was the extent to which she was self-critical. She was for ever striving to improve her work with the result that early attempts were rejected. In fact she later made the comment that if during her time in Staithes she had had the ability reached later in life then she could have done more justice to the environment and the nature of life in the Yorkshire fishing village she so loved.

Hannah Mayor (née Hoyland) 1871-1947

The elopement

It is difficulty after a hundred years to fully appreciate the social relationships that must have existed between the members of the group and the fishing community or within the Staithes Group itself. Other than the two autobiographies written many years later by Laura Knight, there is very little written evidence one can use to capture the spirit which held the group together for about fifteen years. We know that the men enjoyed playing football together and Laura records that there was a warm relationship between the wives of the artists, especially in her case with Henry Hopwood and Fred Jackson's wives.

But one can imagine the excitement that must have circulated in 1902 and 1903 when the Mayors and then the Knights decided to get married although in each case the marriage wasn't to be held in Staithes.

Hannah Hoyland and Fred Mayor had to resort to eloping to London to be married in 1902 as Hannah's father forbade her to marry a 'penniless artist', They settled in Montreuil-sur-Mer in France, this escape being made possible through the kindness of Hannah's cousin the actress Edith Wynne Mathison who lent them £10 for the cost of the journey to Normandy.

The Mayors remained in Montreuil-sur-Mer until 1908 when they decided to return to Whitchurch in Buckinghamshire with the two sons born in France, Freddy and Charles. Yet during their period on the continent the Mayors remained in touch with the Staithes members and were visited by Frederic Stuart Richardson, Henry Silkstone Hopwood and Fred Jackson.

Hannah was then to suffer two tragedies which resulted in her abandoning painting for quite a period. In 1916 at the age of only 49, Frederick died following a botched operation and then in the following year her second son Charles died at about the age of 12.

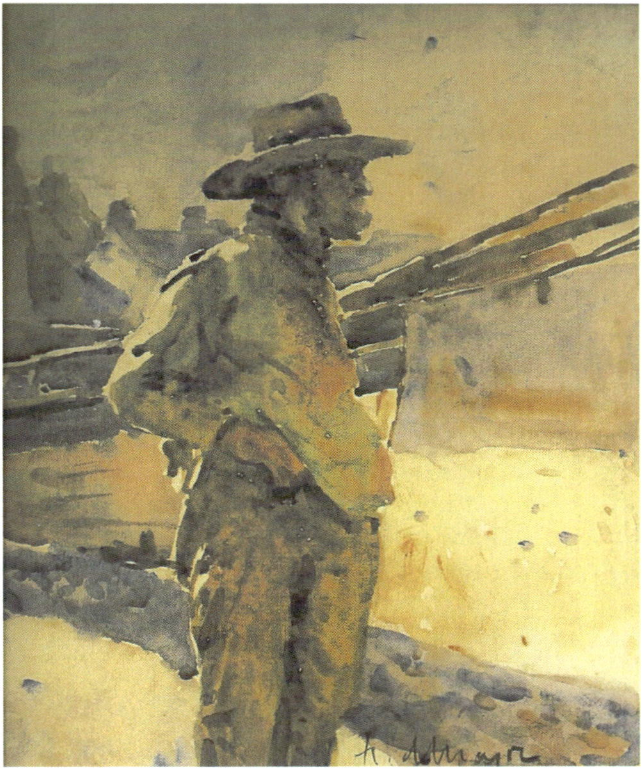

Courtesy of the Pannett Art Gallery, Whitby

After the Great War she did resume her painting especially vases of flowers which had always been a theme she enjoyed. She had exhibited at the Royal Academy in 1904 while living in France and again in 1918 after the cessation of hostilities, she exhibited an oil painting of flowers in the Royal Academy.

Hannah's elder son Freddy (1903-1973) established the Mayor Art Gallery in Cork Street, London, a centre for prestigious art exhibitions.

Hannah's watercolour drawings were similar to Fred Mayor's though not as loose as his could be. In the example in the Pannett Art Gallery *'Fisherman and Coble'* by using a limited palette she has created not only a sense of anxiety as the fisherman peers out to sea deep in his thoughts but also she has given the whole composition uniformity through the dominance of the use of yellow and red ochre.

"Three Men in a Boat"

Jerome K. Jerome's title "Three Men in a Boat" is most apt when discussing the maritime paintings of Ernest Dade, Joseph Richard Bagshawe and Frank Mason. Whereas other members of the Staithes Group seem to have directed much of their attention to the local farming community and the labour of the fields, Dade, Bagshawe and Mason's prime interest was ships and the men who went down to the sea in their ships. Both Dade and Mason spent part of their early life at sea. Dade was a deckhand on the American yacht 'Dauntless' and many years later when he had become a member of the Staithes Art Club he became part-owner of a fishing boat called 'North Star' which they had rigged up as a yacht. It became a floating studio for them with the advantage that *en plein air* to Dade meant plying up and down the Yorkshire coast.

Mason after studying at HMS Conway, the land based naval school in Birmingham, had to apply his knowledge to a term at sea. In the case of Bagshawe, the sea was so irresistible that he bought his own yacht and took every opportunity to join the local fishing fleet as they headed out to the fishing grounds of the North Sea.

The intense interest of these three men in the local fishing boats resulted in Ernest Dade publishing in 1933 his many sketches in his book *'Sail and Oar'*. As a result of Joseph Richard Bagshawe having left sufficient material, his son Gerard Wilfrid Bagshawe produced his father's drawings in *'The Wooden Ships of Whitby'* which was published in the same year of 1933. Beyond doubt, if Bagshawe had not suffered from such an untimely death at the age of 39, I am sure he too would have published in a composite form the many articles he had written for the 'Field' magazine and the 'Yachting and Boating Monthly'.

Mason and Dade's maritime interest was not confined to the fishing village of Staithes. This extract from the minutes of a committee meeting of the Scarborough Sailing Club held on the 5th April, 1904 and which was held at Frank Mason's own studio on Marine Parade, Scarborough, has this reference to Ernest Dade. *'At the meeting, J.B.Butterfield retired as Captain and Ernest Dade was once again elected to fill this position (he was the first Captain in 1895). Most of the business attended to at the meeting focused on an agreement to send several boats to the Royal Yorkshire Yacht Club Regatta at Bridlington in July.'*

This dispels any notion that the members of the Staithes Art Club centred all their time and energy in the fishing village. Each member seems to have had their own degree of commitment.

Ernest Dade 1864-1935

Dade was born in Kensington, London in 1864 but in 1874 the family moved to Scarborough on the Yorkshire coast and so he must have then considered himself a Scarborian. In 1889 after having completed his training as an artist including studying at the Académie Julian in Paris he returned to Scarborough and in 1891 he became one of the founder members of the Staithes Art Club though his affinity with Scarborough remained. To confirm this love for Scarborough and the Yorkshire coast he had his ashes scattered from the end of Scarborough pier into the North Sea which he had so loved.

Dade didn't get married until 1913 just before the outbreak of the Great War when he moved with his new bride to St. John's Wood, London, a studio which in time was taken over by Laura Knight.

Dade characteristically gave his maritime scenes a low horizon, very much as Friedenson often had a low horizon in his landscapes.

He captured the various moods of the sea and whenever he included fishing craft; one has the sense of correctness in all the details of the contour of the vessel and its rigging. This is very evident in the illustration on the front cover where Dade has portrayed a Lowestoft herring drifter in full sail.

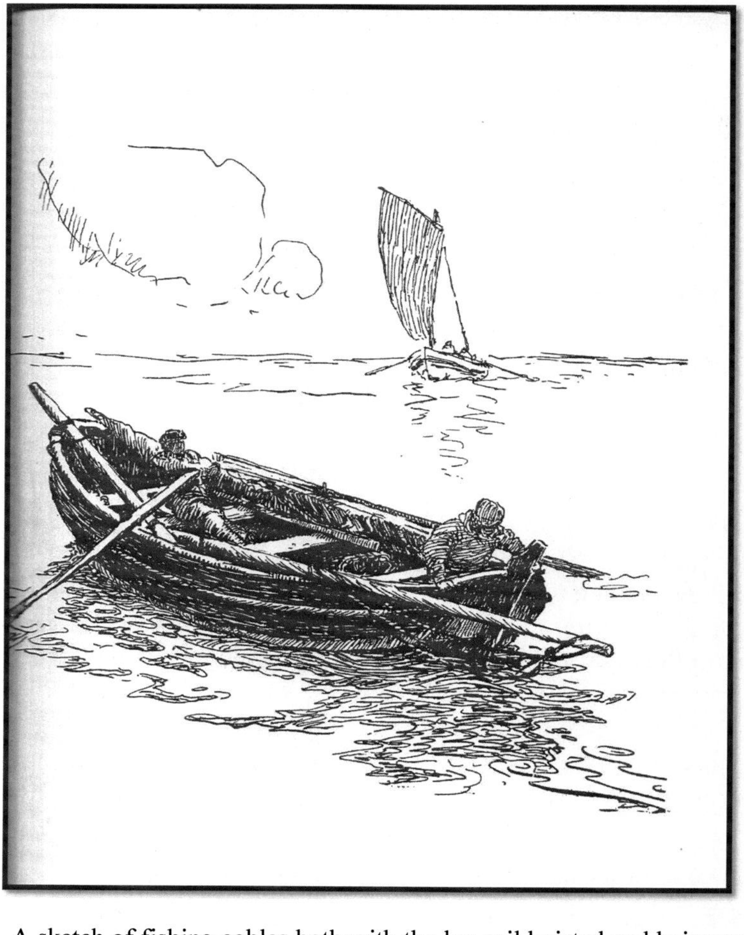

A sketch of fishing cobles both with the lug sail hoisted and being rowed. This is one of the illustrations in Ernest Dade's book 'Sail and Oar' which he published in 1933.

Richard Joseph Bagshawe 1870-1909

There are times when considering the premature death of a great composer, poet or artist, one ponders, 'if only they had lived longer'. If only Mozart had not died at 35 or Schubert at 31, how many more symphonies would have been composed? If Shelley had not died at 29 or Keats aged 25, how much richer would English literature have been? If Turner' exact contemporary Thomas Girton had not died at the age of 27, would Turner have been right in predicting that Girton would have been a greater artist than himself?

With Joseph Richard Bagshawe, who died at the age of 39, we can only conjecture how great his contribution could have been to the history of art if he had completed the biblical three score years and ten.

His paintings, many of which portray the hazards of launching cobles into a fierce North Sea, display a masterly use of colour, movement, tension and above all accuracy in every detail of the vessels.

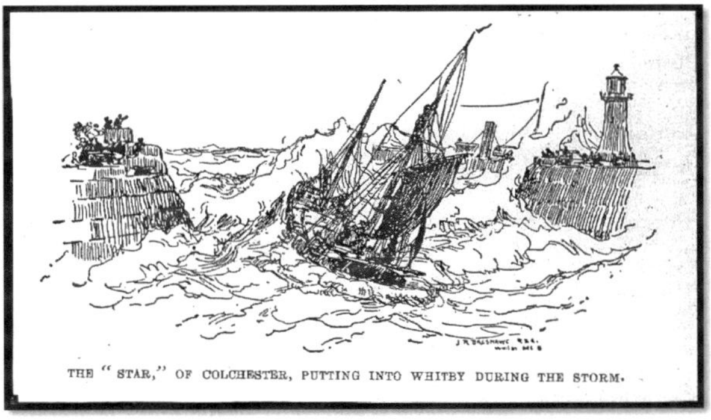

Sketch from Bagshawe's "Wooden Ships of Whitby"

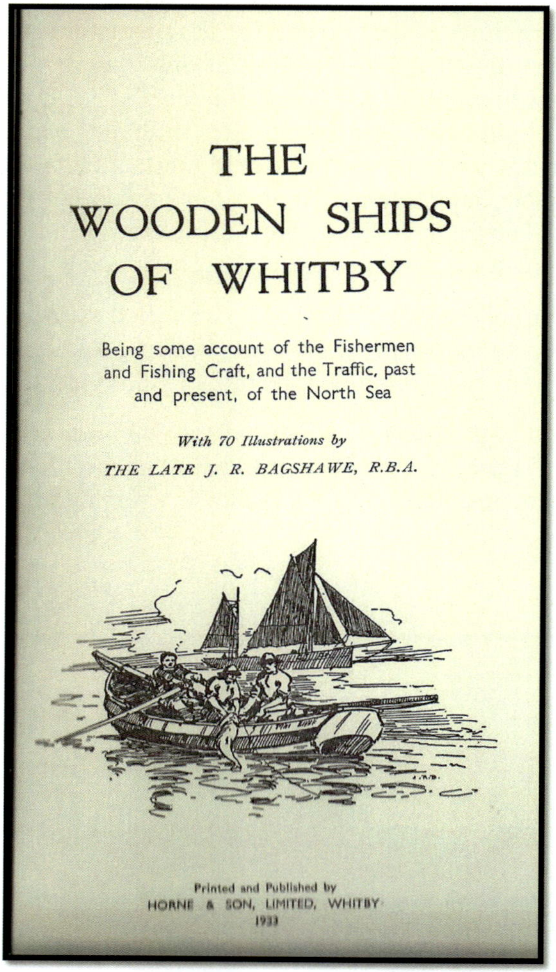

THE
WOODEN SHIPS
OF WHITBY

Being some account of the Fishermen
and Fishing Craft, and the Traffic, past
and present, of the North Sea

With 70 Illustrations by

THE LATE J. R. BAGSHAWE, R.B.A.

Printed and Published by
HORNE & SON, LIMITED, WHITBY
1933

This the title page of ‘Wooden Ships of Whitby’ which was published by Joseph Richard Bagshawe’s son in 1933.

Like Frank Mason, Bagshawe found a source of income in producing paintings to be used in the production of the humble postcard to cater for the ever increasing number of visitors. In the case of Bagshawe, he had a contract with the premier postcard producer Tuck and Son. This did much to enhance his reputation as a marine artist.

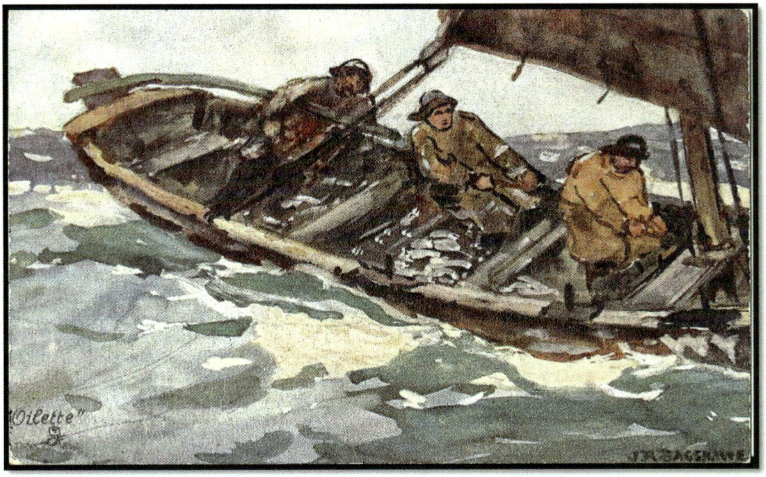

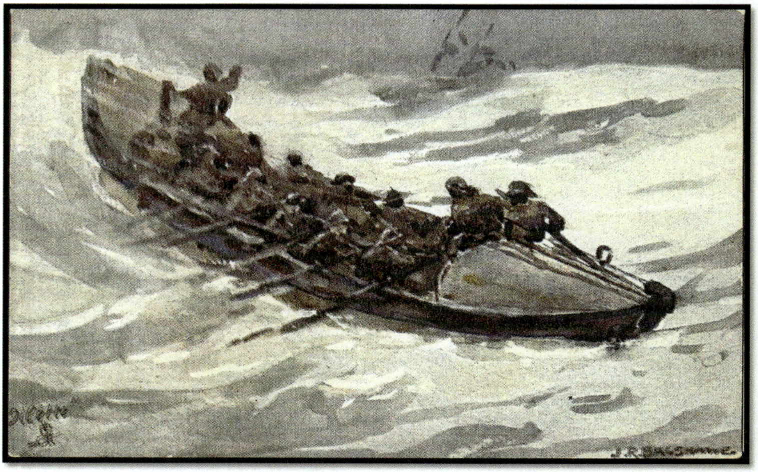
J R BAGSHAWE

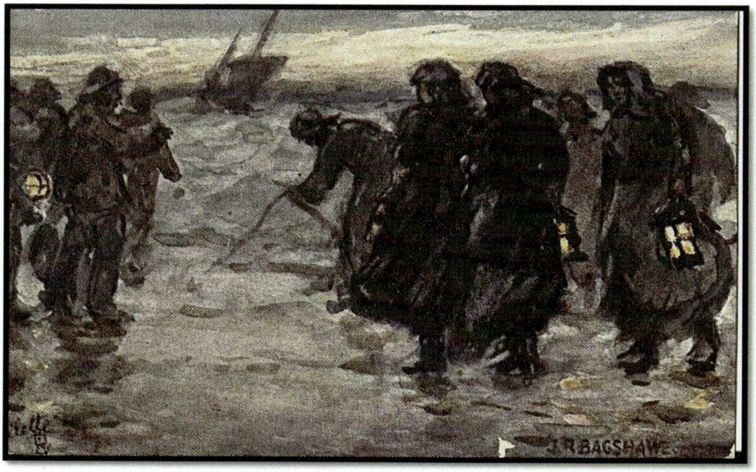
J R BAGSHAWE

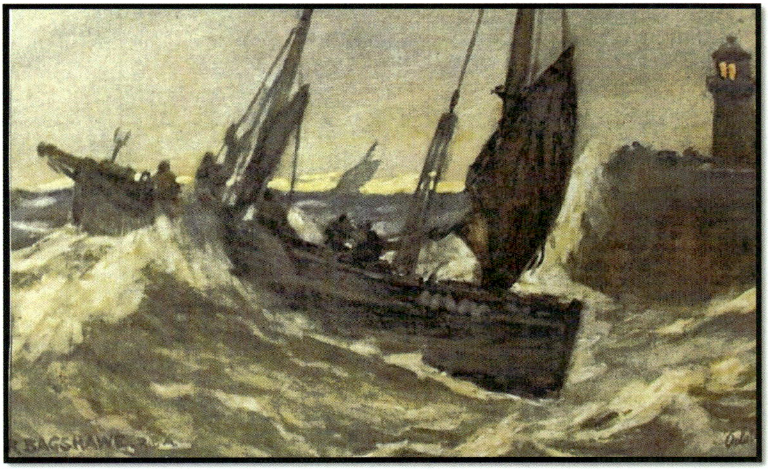

Four postcards from the Raphael Tuck's Oilette Series 'Toilers of the Sea'.

The paintings are by Joseph Richard Bagshawe

Frank Henry Mason 1876-1965

When discussing the life and work of Frank Mason it is tempting to forget that this study is designed to cover the period 1894 to 1909. Frank Mason is now mainly remembered for the work he was to produce later. In the 1920's he concentrated on graphic art and produced a large corpus of engravings and posters for the railway carriages of the London North Eastern Railway company and other railway and shipping agencies.. Even before the dissolution of the Staithes Group, Mason had his paintings reproduced by the Scarborough firm of E.T.W. Dennis & Son, Ltd.

Mason was born in Seaton Carew in County Durham in October 1876 but his training in art, which was his main passion, did not materialise until, like Ernest Dade, he moved to live in Scarborough. Once settled there he entered the well respected Scarborough School of

Art where he came under the influence of the head of the school, Albert Strange. Strange had been appointed head in 1882 and retained this position until his death in 1917. For Mason this proved to be a double blessing for Albert Strange was a keen yachtsman and yacht designer and so the two men shared common interests. Albert Strange was also the founder of the Scarborough Yacht Club of which both Frank Mason and Ernest Dade became actively engaged.

Mason, like Dade and Bagshawe was a founder member of the Staithes Art Club in 1901 and so these 'Three Men in a Boat', as it were, became responsible for the main maritime output of the Staithes Group. Other members on occasion may have captured the fishing fleet as it set out on its quest for the harvest of fish but for Mason, Dade and Bagshawe, the sea meant everything.

During his time with the Staithes Group, Mason actively promoted his paintings through several exhibitions. In 1900 he exhibited in the Royal Academy, he submitted works in each of the annual exhibitions of the Staithes Art Club and in 1905, he even included his works in the rival Anderson's Rembrandt Gallery while the rest of the club had to use the small exhibition hall in Waterloo Place.

The Royal Hotel on the promenade in Whitby has several fine paintings by Frank Mason which he actually painted directly onto the wall of the main lounge. These are a fine reminder of Mason's association with this part of Yorkshire.

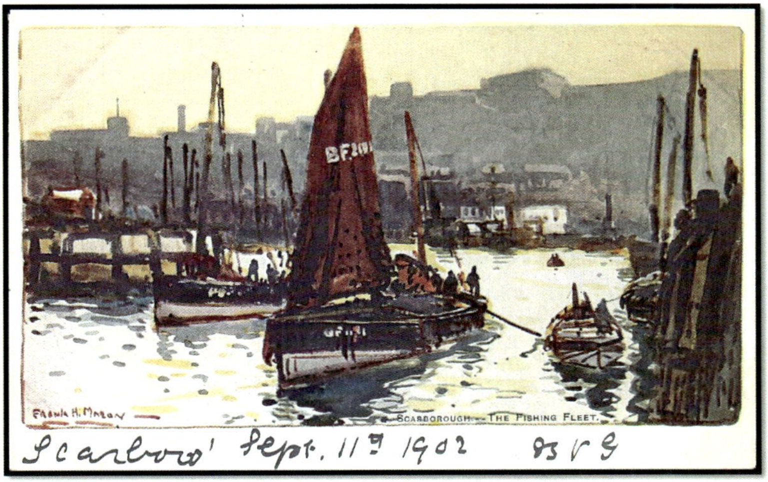

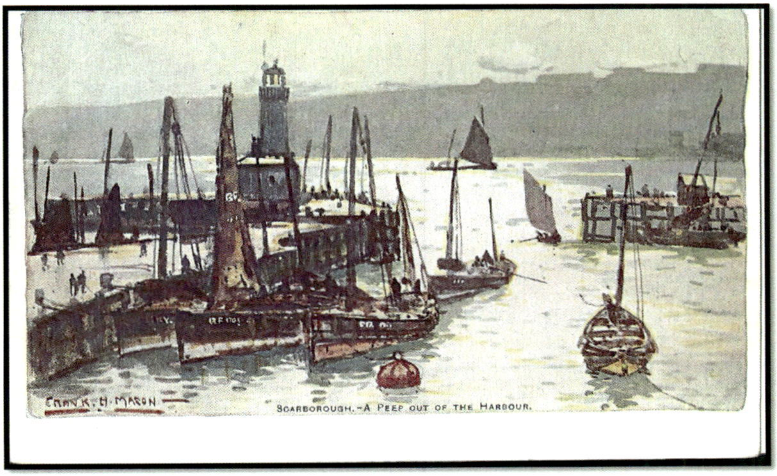

Two postcards taken from paintings by Frank Mason dated 1902

The Equestrian Duo

James William Booth 1867-1953

Booth attended the Manchester School of Art under the tutorship of Elias Bancroft. In 1898 he exhibited at the Royal Academy and also he constantly submitted work to the Royal Cambrian Academy.

Elias Bancroft 1846-1924 had produced several oil paintings of Whitby and perhaps in conjunction with Booth's friendship with Fred Jackson, he was encouraged in 1901 to move to the Yorkshire Coast. Like Dade and Mason, Booth decided to be based in Scarborough and chose a house in the village of Scalby called Haswell. One of the first things Booth did was to build a studio in the garden though when he became associated with the Staithes Group, he later shared a studio with Harold Knight.

Booth was nominated and received membership of the Staithes Art Club in 1902. Distance from Staithes was not a problem for him as the village of Scalby had its own railway station on the direct route from Scarborough to Staithes.

I've classed Booth under the heading 'The Equestrian Duo' because like John Atkinson, so many of the canvases he produced are portraits of Shire Horses, or the local breed, the Cleveland Bay. When the horses are the main feature of the painting, the work was given a title such as '*The Draught Horse*', '*End O'Day*', '*Ploughing Horse*', '*Homeward Bound*' or '*A Country Horse Show*' and even when Booth recorded a scene of work, he would include a horse or horse and cart in some way such as in the paintings '*The Quarry*', '*Fish Sales*' or '*Carting Sand*'.

James William Booth died on the 18th August 1953 at the age of 85.

John Atkinson 1863-1924

Atkinson was born in Newcastle, a city with a continuous tradition of painting. He was tutored by Wilson Hepple while he attended the Newcastle School of Art and then, like the Joblings, he was drawn south by the news of the vibrant activity that existed among the Staithes Group of Artists.

Between 1900 and 1914, the main years of activity in Staithes, he lived in Sleights near Whitby and then he moved to Glaisdale to the house called Broadleas. In 1914 he returned to Newcastle where he set up his studio and continued painting his horse studies until his death in 1924. He was buried in Saltwell Cemetery in Gateshead.

Atkinson's first of ten pictures he prepared for the Royal Academy was executed while he lived Sleights and he also exhibited at the Royal Scottish Academy. His ability was recognised when he was elected a member of the Staithes Art Club in 1907.

Atkinson taught at Ushaw College and the Grammar School in Morpeth.

Owen Bowen 1873-1967

Owen Bowen was born in Beeston in Leeds and after attending the local High School, he enrolled at the Leeds School of Art. It was there that he became associated with William Gilbert Foster and through this connection a friendship developed which eventually resulted in his being elected a member of the Staithes Art Club in 1904. Bowen frequently included his work in the club's annual exhibitions. Although based in Leeds, he usually spent his summers on the Yorkshire coast and especially at Robin Hood's Bay.

Bowen had special expertise at painting still life compositions and a characteristic of his many flower studies was the iridescence he applied to the glass vases which often complemented the prime colours of the flower heads.

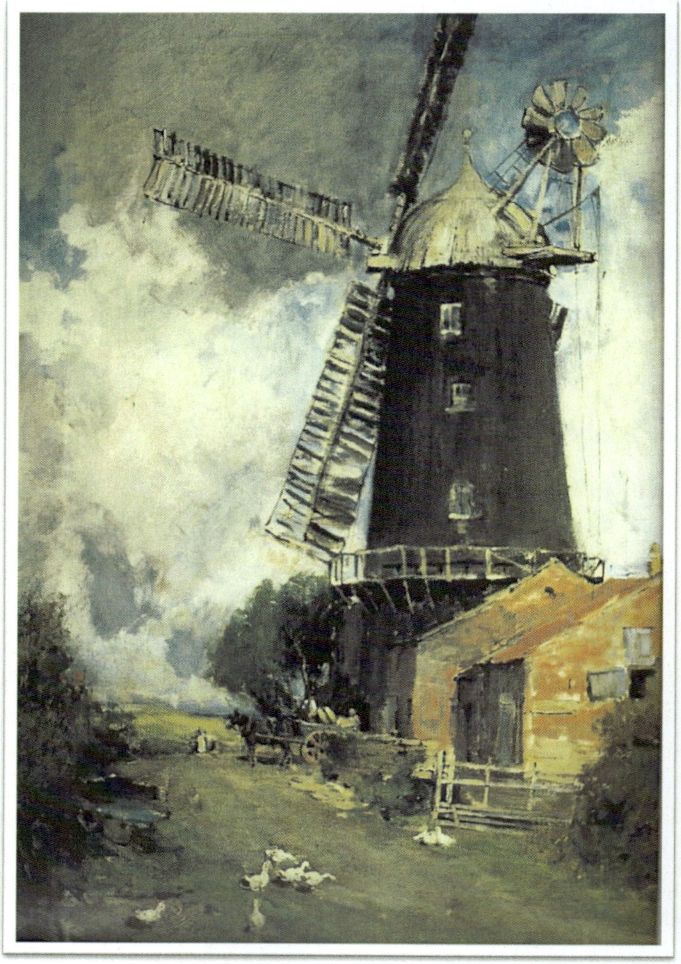

'Hawsker Mill' Owen Bowen. Courtesy of the Pannett Art Gallery, Whitby

Generally speaking, his earlier works are inclined to be superior and do not have the 'looseness' found in some of his later paintings. He was quite prolific and with his longevity it means that his works are often to be found.

Examples of his oils are to be seen in most of the Yorkshire art galleries. He also exhibited at the Royal Academy, the Royal Institute of Painters in Oils, the Royal Cambrian Academy, the Walker Gallery to name just a few of the venues used by him.

Owen died at East Keswick, having attained the age of ninety-three.

Lionel Townsend Crawshaw 1864-1949

Lionel Townsend Crawshaw was born on the 5th of April, 1864 at Warmsworth, a small village near to Doncaster. After attending Doncaster Grammar School and the Society of Friends school of St. Peter's in York, he trained for the legal profession at Christ College, Cambridge. But his desire to paint led him to study at the Académie Colorossi in Paris and also in Germany at Dusseldorf and Karlsruhe.

Like so many young British artists towards the close of the 19th century who wished to pursue a more avant-garde approach to art as practised in the coastal artist colonies, Crawshaw decided to move to Whitby where he rented a studio. He became a member of the Staithes Art Club in 1904, the same year as Owen Bowen. Although he later moved to Edinburgh, Liverpool, Droitwich and Devon, he retained his Whitby studio for 40 years.

Crawshaw first exhibited at the Royal Academy in 1907 and continued to forward works for selection until 1946. His paintings possessed a high degree of realism and covered a wide range of genre.

His second wife Frances Fisher, whom he married in 1930, was also a painter.

Lionel Crawshaw died on the 16th of March, 1949 in Newton Abbot just prior to his 85th birthday.

Arthur A. Friedenson 'Friedi' 1872-1955

What makes a great artist?

I suppose one could write a book trying to answer this question and still fail to do it justice. But there is one feature which seems to be a characteristic of all great artists and this is the ability to enable the viewer to recognise the identity of the creator of the work. This is true whether one is looking at a portrait by Rembrandt or Van Gogh, a sculpture by Michelangelo or Henry Moore or a landscape of Monet or David Hockney.

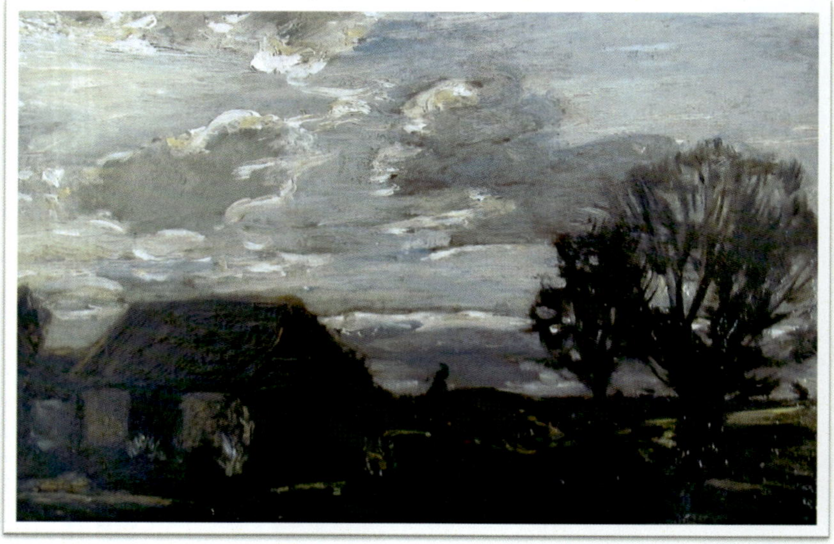

From a private collection

Arthur Friedenson's work has its own identity which sets it apart from the rest of the Staithes Group and which shows his maturity of style and confidence in execution. These features are well illustrated in this oil painting. Firstly he often chose to use a low horizon such as in this example where the landmass uses only a quarter of the canvas. Secondly he was prone to use a heavy treatment of the foreground which requires the viewer to carefully observe the range of his palette in this area. Finally, and this is his hallmark, he leaves a wide area of sky so he could capture his characteristic cloud formations with their distinctive white linings.

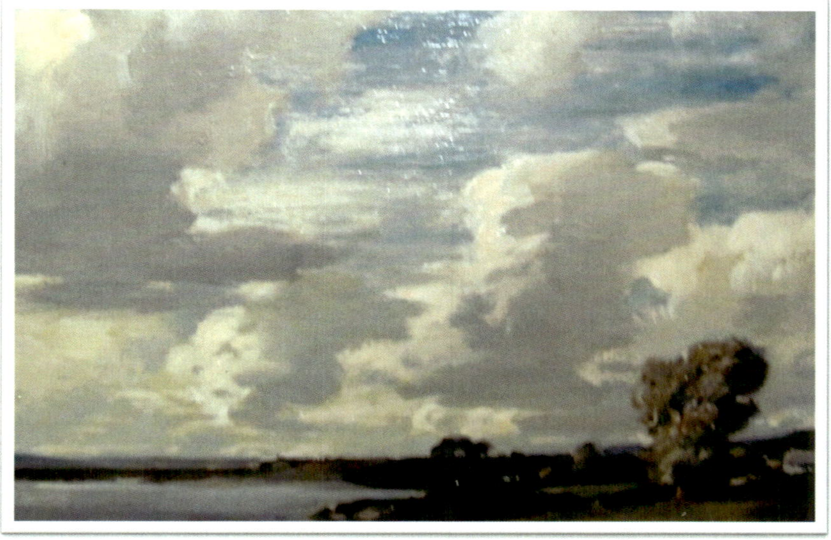

Courtesy of the Pannett Art Gallery, Whitby

There is a danger in psychoanalysing a painting but the repetition of this treatment by Friedenson has caused some to suggest that his forbidding foreground captures his own forebodings whereas the rays of light which frame his cloud formations captures more a sense of hope and optimism. Whether this is the case or not, these elements enable us to differentiate his work from the rest of the Staithes Group.

When it comes to compiling a biographical outline for Arthur Friedenson's origins one finds various opinions but it appears he stemmed from a Jewish/North European parentage and that he was born in the North of England – possibly Leeds in 1872. (For those with an interest in genealogy, there is quite a challenge here in investigating Friedenson's background and possible connection with Russia.)

His first employment was as a sign writer but his precocious ability resulted in his painting *'Departing Day'* being accepted at the Royal Academy when he was only 17 years of age. According to the records of the Yorkshire Union of Artists, of which he was a Vice President for many years from 1908, he submitted over 50 paintings to the RA up to 1938 when he ceased to produce any further works.

Like several other artists who later joined the Staithes Group, Friedenson decided in 1890 to attend the Académie Julian in Paris to become acquainted with all the latest movements in the art world. His remained at the Académie Julian until 1892. He then moved to the Académie Royale des Beaux-Arts in Antwerp. In 1896 he decided to return to the Académie Julian and it was during these continental visits that he met Henry Silkstone Hopwood which was to prove an important contact for after his second term in Paris, Friedenson decided to move to Staithes where he shared lodgings with Harold Knight and Fred Mayor. Friedenson is included in the 1901 list of founder members of the Staithes Art Club.

An important event during his time at Staithes was when in 1908 his oil painting *'Runswick Bay'* was purchased for the nation by the Chantrey Bequest and now is in the permanent collection of the Tate Gallery.

In 1908 Friedenson moved to Wareham and later Corfe Castle in Dorset where he continued to produce paintings for most of the important galleries in the country but from the point of view of this study, his connection with the Staithes Group had come to an end.

He died at Parkstone in Dorset in 1955 aged 82 but he will be remembered always for the large corpus of paintings he produced during his very eventful life.

Robert Jobling 1841-1923

Though the artist colonies around the British coastline at the close of the 19th century were usually isolated fishing villages, nevertheless, there was awareness between them of the work each was producing. This was no more evident than in the case of the Cullercoates group and those painting further south in the Yorkshire fishing village of Staithes.

Isa Thompson and Robert Jobling were both accomplished artists grounded in the Cullercoates tradition but they both moved later from Cullercoates to become members of the Staithes Art Club, Robert Jobling in the foundation year of the club in 1901 and Isa Thompson the following year.

Robert previously had been an active promoter of exhibitions and founder of art societies in Northumberland. He was instrumental in setting up the Newcastle Life School in 1878, organising the first exhibition of the Borough of Tynemouth Art Club in 1883, was Vice President of the Bewick Club and involved in the establishing of Newcastle's fine Laing Art Gallery in 1904.

In 1892 tragically Robert's wife Annie died leaving him with four children but in the following year Robert married Isa Thompson whom he'd known for many years through their Cullercoates connection, and like the Mayors and the Knights, Robert and Isa Jobling became married members of the Staithes Art Club.

A characteristic of Jobling's paintings was his versatility. He was as perfectly at home painting the launching of the Staithes cobles from the shoreline as he was in the countryside recording the annual routine of the farming community. Jobling's paintings from his Staithes period always have a sense of having been created *en plein air*. There is a constant freshness about them.

Often to animate a scene he would include a group of women either as they gaze anxiously out to sea waiting for the safe arrival of their loved ones or helping in the preparation for the fishermen's departure. The sway of their black skirts in the wind gives his paintings a sense of reality. A fine example of this is '*When the Boats Come In*' which was shown at the Royal Academy in 1883. A group of three women are holding empty wickerwork baskets as they stand on the beach waiting to transport the fish from the cobles which had just arrived. Another fine example is '*Harbour Scene with Fishermen*' in the Laing Art Gallery collection. Here two Staithes women wearing their traditional bonnets talk to a fisherman beside his coble.

Jobling was a constant exhibitor at each of the Staithes Art Club's annual exhibitions and the Whitby Gazette reports show that he submitted a wide range of subjects including paintings he had executed while staying in Holland. He is rightly classed as one of the main contributors to the ever growing reputation of the Staithes Group of Artists.

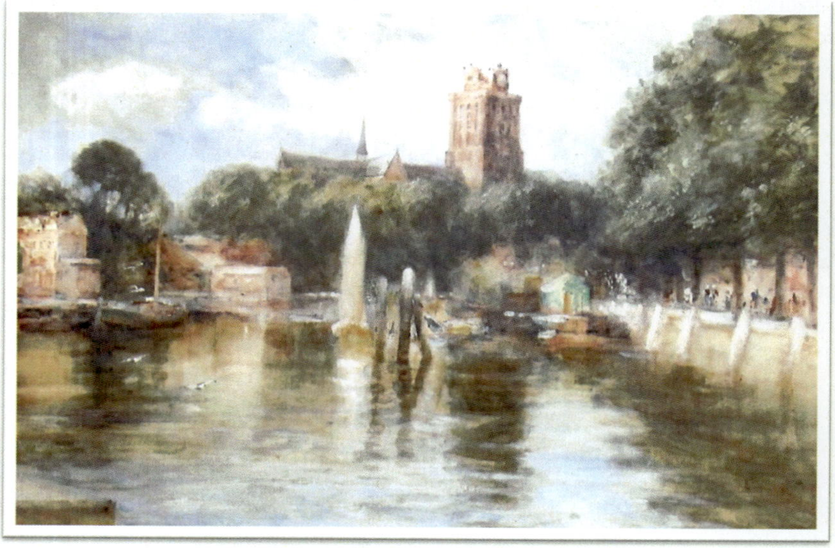

Dordrecht Holland. Private collection

This watercolour of Dordrecht in Holland which Jobling painted in 1903, illustrates the extent of his exposure to the impressionist movement. The yacht in full sail in the centre of the composition has been treated with a minimum of brush strokes. The foliage of the trees on the right have an almost stipple effect and there is the slightest hint of people on the embankment.. The painting could easily have been created by a member of the French Impressionists. It is a large watercolour measuring 50 mm. by 37 mm. It also shows his skill in using a difficult medium for such a large surface area. His sense of colour was always a hallmark of Jobling's work.

Henry Silkstone Hopwood 1860-1914

Henry Silkstone Hopwood was born in Markfield near Leicester on the 12th of January, 1860. His parents soon moved to Manchester and so when he wanted to study art he enrolled at the Manchester School of Art. Like many young men he had the wander lust and from 1888 to 1890 he became a globe trotter as a deck hand which enabled him to visit such places as Australia and Japan.

From 1890 to 1891 he continued his studies first at the Académie Julian in Paris where he was tutored by Bouguereau and then at the Academy in Antwerp where he met Arthur Friedenson.

1894 was a milestone year for Hopwood for his watercolour *'Industry'*, which was on show at the Royal Academy, was bought for the nation under the Chantry Bequest.

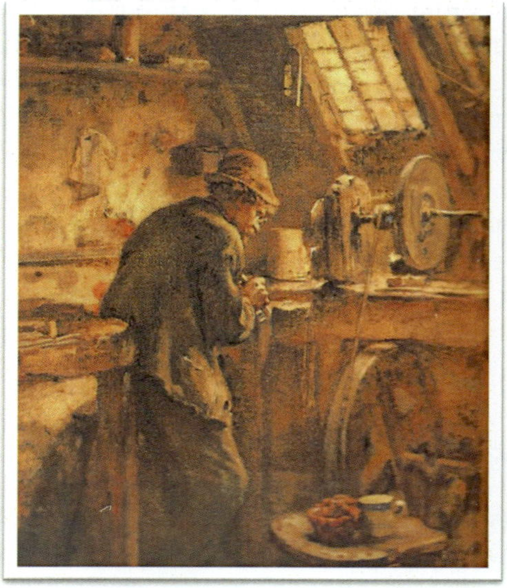

The Jet Worker   Henry Silkstone Hopwood.

Courtesy of the Pannett Art Gallery, Whitby

He built his house in Hinderwell in 1900 and the following year he was appointed chairman of the newly inaugurated Staithes Art Club and became an active member even including visiting the Mayors in Normandy and Spence Ingall In Tangiers.

Hopwood had a special fondness for watercolours and was made a member of the RWS in 1908. He died in Edinburgh on the 26th of September, 1914 aged 54.

Henry Rowland Hill 1873-1952

Hill was one of the few members of the Staithes Group who decided to continue living in the Staithes area after the group finally disbanded in 1909. When he married Dorothy Turner in 1908, they decided to settle in Ellerby, a small hamlet near Runswick and Hinderwell and he remained there submitting entries into the Royal Academy until his final painting in 1940. It was a remarkable 44 years since his first paintings *'Primrose Gatherers'* and *'Blackberry Gathering'* were accepted by the Royal Academy in 1896.

Hill was born in Halifax and trained at the Halifax School of Art and also at the Art School at the Bradford Technical College. The prime influence upon Hill was in 1895 when he studied at Bushey in Hertfordshire under Sir Hubert von Herkomer which resulted in his visiting Bavaria with von Herkomer in 1896 and again in 1897.

Rowland Hill was a founder member of the Staithes Art Club being elected in 1901 and continually exhibited at the club's annual exhibitions both in Staithes and then in Whitby. He produced a large quantity of works in both oils and watercolours but he seems to have preferred using watercolours. In his later work there is a varying degree of quality but his sense of colour was a prime characteristic of all his output with the result that his paintings always have a sense of freshness.

Besides the normal subject matter found among the paintings of the Staithes Group, Hill seemed to have had a special interest in abbeys and other ruined ecclesiastical buildings. This may be because he lived so near to the ruined Benedictine abbey in Whitby.

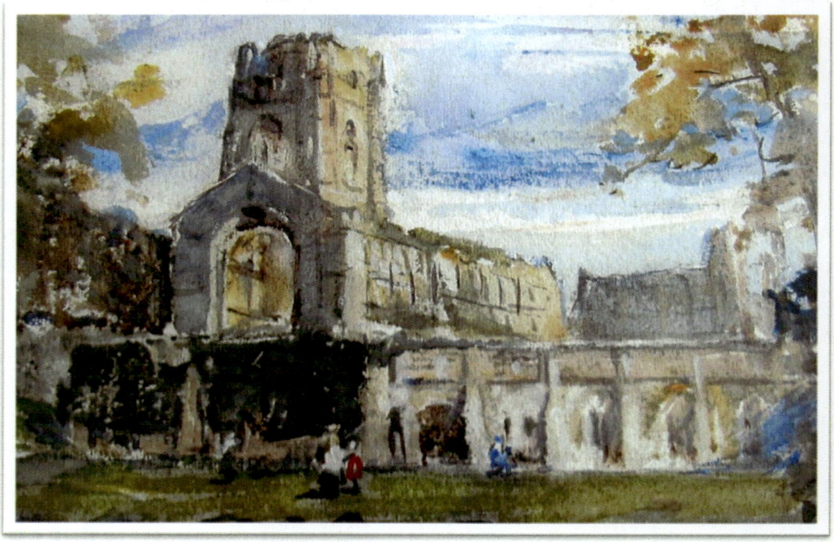

Fountains Abbey 1909 Private collection

Henry Rowland Hill was a distant relative of his namesake, the Post Office reformer who introduced Uniform Penny Postage in 1840. Hill was also interested in philately and published a book on the subject.

Harold Knight 1874-1961

'Harold, the best critic I have known who never forces his own point of view on other painters, but considers rather if the effort is sincere. Harold's gift of understanding comes possibly through his extraordinary sensitive and sympathetic nature.'

In these words from her first autobiography, *'Oil Paint and Grease Paint'*, Laura Knight encapsulates the personality of Harold – a person sensitive and sympathetic.

Harold was born in Nottingham in 1847. His artistic gift was soon evident and after studying at the Nottingham School of Art, where he was to meet his future wife the fellow student Laura Johnson, he went to Paris to study at the renowned Académie Julian. Harold was Laura's senior both in age and initially in training and later she records how she would stand behind him as he painted trying to copy identically the work he was undertaking.

Harold's first visit to Staithes was with Laura, her sister and aunt and it was then that he first developed an affinity with the fishing village. Harold and Laura, who became his wife in 1903 during their Staithes period, visited Holland in 1904 and 1905 which greatly helped him as he developed his skill as a portrait painter.

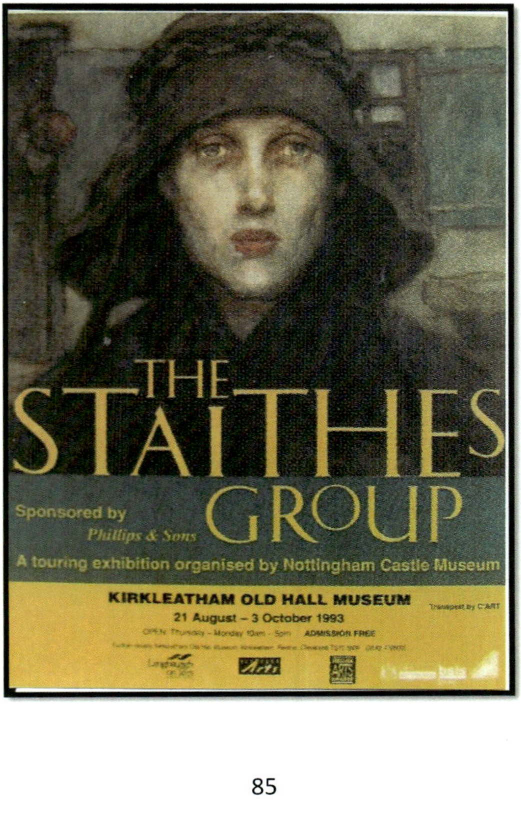

Perhaps the most iconic painting to come from the whole of the work of the Staithes Group was this paintng by Harold of a young bereaved fisherwoman. Framed by her black mourning bonnet, he has captured the depth of her grief. She seems to have instantly aged, her hollow cheeks symbolise the emptiness within her as she faces her future loneliness. In this 1993 poster, the Nottingham Castle Museum chose this poignant image to capture the arduous life the fisherfolk of Staithes had to experience and the constant danger faced by the fishermen.

Though Laura was so honoured by being made a Dame of the British Empire and also being only the second woman to be made a Royal Academician, this does not mean that her work was of a higher quality than Harold's. Some art critics would say that Laura's achievements have been inclined to place Harold's work very much in the shadow. Especially during the Staithes period, Harold's work was more accomplished than Laura's and it was not until their move to Newlyn and her time with the circus, the theatre, and with gypsies that the focus was more on her.

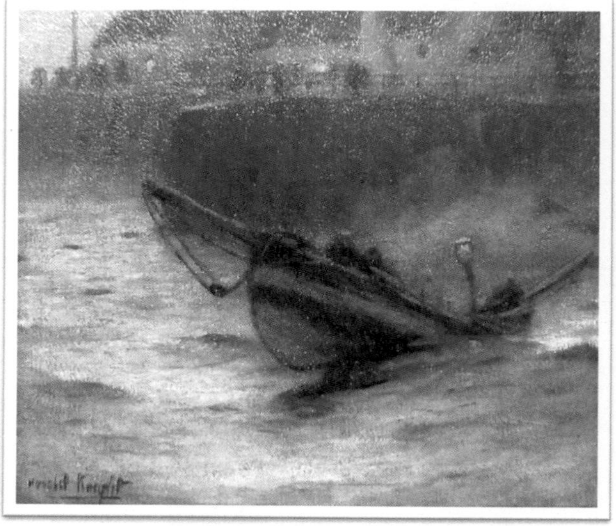

This dramatic oil painting by Harold Knight in the Pannett Gallery, Whitby, which shows a vessel trying the leave the shelter of the staith, is very much in the style of Joseph Richard Bagshawe and possesses all the qualities of an impressionist work. Harold Knight has captured the force of the sea and the vulnerability of the fishing craft.

Harold died in 1961 after a successful career as a portrait painter. He was made a member of the Royal Society of Portrait Painters in 1926 and a Royal Academician in 1937, incidentally, after Laura's elevation to RA.

Charles Hodge Mackie 1862-1920

We have had several connections with the Cullercoates group of artists but with Charles Hodge Mackie there was a link with the progressive activity in Scotland. In 1884 Mackie had established a studio in Edinburgh but following a visit to Whitby in 1900, he decided to base himself at Roxby on the Yorkshire Moors above Staithes. However, he continued to keep his connection with Scotland and in 1901 he was elected a member of the Royal Scottish Society of Painters in Watercolours to be followed by membership of the Royal Scottish Academy in 1917. Yet Mackie still supported the Staithes Art Club and exhibited in their annual exhibition.

Mackie received mention in Laura Knight's autobiography as she benefitted from having had lessons from him.

Charles Hodge Mackie RSA RSW died in 1920 in his beloved Edinburgh.

William Frederick Mayor 1866-1916

Fred Mayor, as he use to sign his work, and Arthur Friedenson though so dissimilar in style did share several things in common. Both were original in their work and both possessed exceptional talent. They both chose to spend several years at the Académie Julian, Friedenson from 1890 to 1892 and a second time in 1896 and Fred Mayor from 1886 for four years. Both artists had the ability to absorb techniques and theories from leading artists yet in doing so each strove to formulate their own distinctive style. Fred Mayor developed a lasting friendships with many established artists including Frank Brangwyn, Philip Wilson Steer, Walter Richard Sickert and Edward Stott and his own development was very much though their influence.

Years later Laura Knight records in her first autobiography that she once chided Fred Mayor for being too dependent upon other artists. '*Fred Mayor made a brilliant showing, but he was full of tricks that he had picked up here, there and everywhere. Some of his watercolours were quite lovely, and he had a beautiful colour sense when he forgot the Stotts the Brangwyns and the Melvilles he was so constantly imitating.*'

After his years of study on the continent where he had been exposed to the latest developments in Impressionism, Fred Mayor moved to Staithes in 1899. He shared lodgings with Arthur Friedenson and Harold Knight in the home of Mr. and Mrs. George Porritt in Gun Gutter and at the institution of the Staithes Art Club in 1901 he became one of the twenty founder members.

Unfortunately his stay in Staithes was short lived for in 1902 when he and Hannah Hoyland decided that they would like to get married, her father emphatically refused to give his consent. So strong was his opposition that Fred and Hannah fled to London where they were married before crossing the Channel to settle in Montreuil-sur-Mer. Though far from the centre of activity in Staithes, he still kept contact with the members, was visited in France by Frederic Stuart Richardson, Henry Silkstone Hopwood and Fred Jackson and he himself journeyed to Tangiers to stay with Spence Ingall.

This exile lasted until 1908 when the Mayors returned to England with the two sons who had been born in France and who were soon to be followed by the birth of a daughter.

The Mayors settled in Buckinghamshire where Fred continued to paint and entered his work in many national exhibitions. As early as when he was 21 his painting titled '*Autumn*' was accepted at the Royal Academy. But what promised to be a productive period suddenly came to an end when tragically he died in 1916 at the age of 49 following an unsuccessful operation.

As in the case of Richard Joseph Bagshawe who died when he was only 39, one can only estimate what both these artists could have produced and what an influence they could have had on the development of British art if they had not died so prematurely.

This small watercolour sketch dated 1898 of windmills in Holland illustrates the loose wash on wash technique Mayor used so naturally and successfully. His minimal number of broad brush strokes allowed the pigment to take its own course on the dampened paper with the result that he has produced a fine effect of water reflections. (Unfortunately the watercolour has some foxing which is sometimes found on the paper used by Mayor),

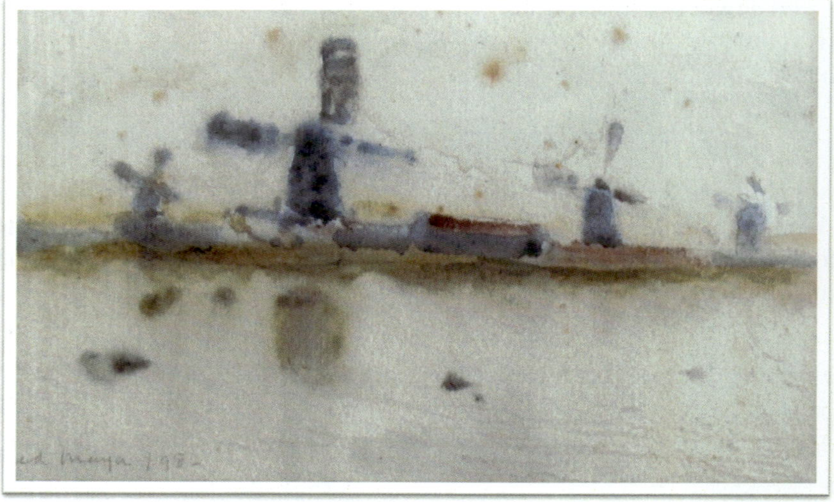

Dutch Windmills Fred Mayor From a private collection

Ernest Higgins Rigg 1868-1947

Ernest Higgins Rigg was born in Bradford, the same city as the composer Frederick Delius who was born there just six years earlier. Ernest's siblings, four brothers and a sister also displayed varying degrees of artistic talent. Albert Herbert, the eldest who was born in 1850, was an accomplished artist and accepted at the Royal Academy. Alfred Edward, who was born in 1870, two years after Ernest Higgins, displayed works at several galleries including the Royal Academy, Grosvenor Gallery and the Walker Gallery in Liverpool.

Ernest started his studies at the Bradford School of Art but like so many future members of the Staithes Group, he spent time at the Académie Julian in Paris acquainting himself with the latest developments in continental art. In 1887 with Rowland Hill he was instrumental in forming the Yorkshire Union of Artists and so when the Staithes Art Club returned to the Union in 1906, it must have given

Ernest a degree of satisfaction. After his training he came to Staithes in 1896 and so was one of the founder members of the group.

Twenty examples of his work were accepted by the Royal Academy including '*With eventide our toil is o'er*', '*The Shadows of Departing Day*' and '*The Coming of Spring*'. Although Ernest Rigg was among a group who spent so much time capturing the life of the fishing community, these Royal Academy works illustrate how he preferred to capture the rural life of the hinterland of Staithes. He was much happier painting a Friesen cow than capturing the contours of a local coble fishing boat. But this illustrates independence within the Staithes Art Club which was partly due to the fact that there was no specific leader as was the case at Newlyn or among the Glasgow Boys.

The recent publication of '*The Secret Staithes Diary of Enid Lucy Pearse Robinson*' prompted Ernest Rigg's daughter Darnley Rigg to challenge some of the images of her father portrayed by the diarist. She also used the opportunity to give some insight into Ernest's personality and motivation.

'My memories of him, include a man wrapped up in, and dedicated to his work, if a serious turn of mind, though he could be sociable and animated when the occasion called for it. In fact, so few of his paintings was executed in Staithes. I assume he preferred socialising rather than working whilst he stayed there!

I would describe him as quite a stern, strict man. He applied himself diligently to his painting and was interested in his art in a comprehensive way.'

Several members of the Staithes Group and especially Owen Bowen produced still life images of vases of flowers. In this example Ernest Rigg has skilfully placed the shadow of the flowers as a background to the right of the vase, thus giving the whole image a 3D effect.

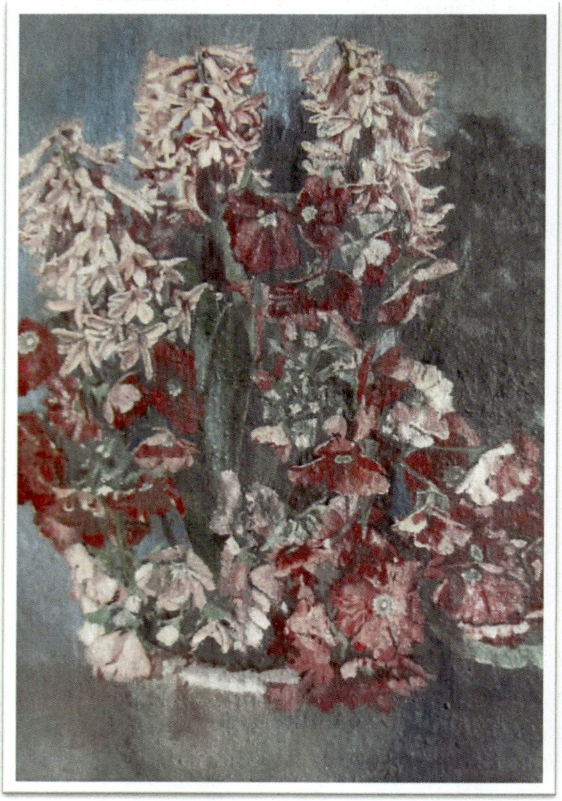

Vase of flowers Private collection

Albert George Stevens 1863-1925

Albert George Stevens was one of the founder members of the Staithes Art Club from 1901. He settled in Whitby in 1902 and was one of the few members who remained in the area after the group dispersed in 1909. He died in Whitby in 1925. Like many members of the group he exhibited several times at the Royal Academy starting with his painting '*Cottage Interior*' which he submitted in 1903. He liked to paint jet workers as they worked at their lathes. Another craftsman he portrayed was Whitby's famous cabinet maker Mr. Varley whose furniture sometimes appears in local auction sales with occasionally a painting by A.G.Stevens himself.

Stevens like Frank Mason and Joseph Bagshawe used the craze for sending postcards in the years leading up the Great War to promote their paintings. A.G.Stevens chose to have his watercolours published as postcards by the Lincoln firm of J.W.Ruddock. They were specialists in this field and also published the paintings of the Robin Hood's Bay artist Ulrich Walmsley (the father of the novelist Leo Walmsley).

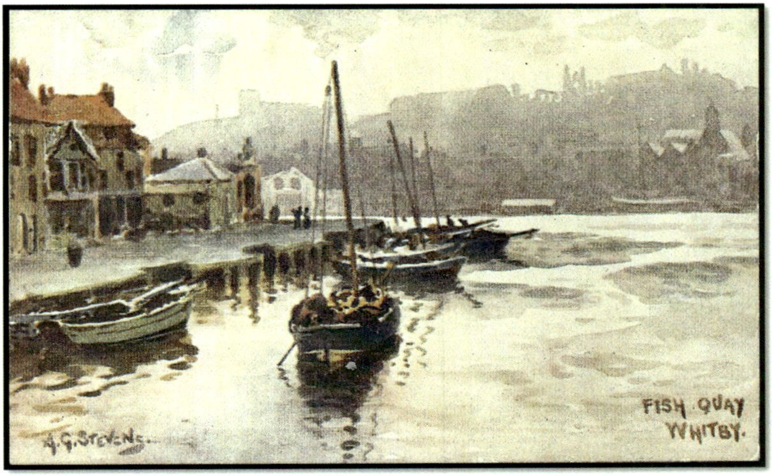

Fish Quay Whitby by A.G.Stevens

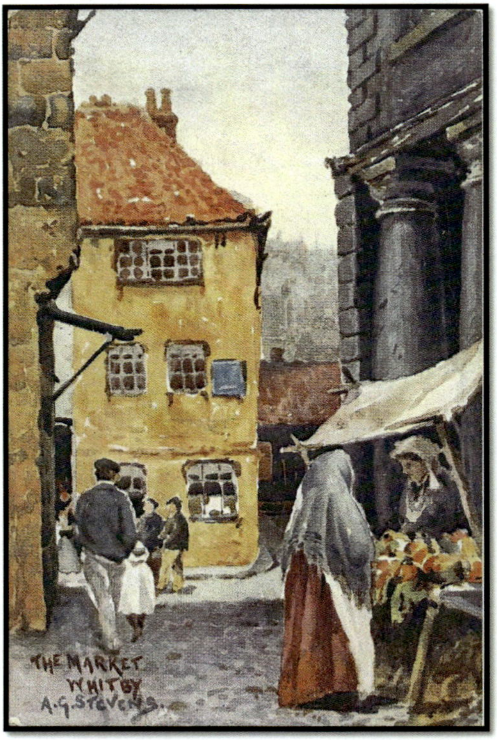

The Market Whitby. A G Stevens

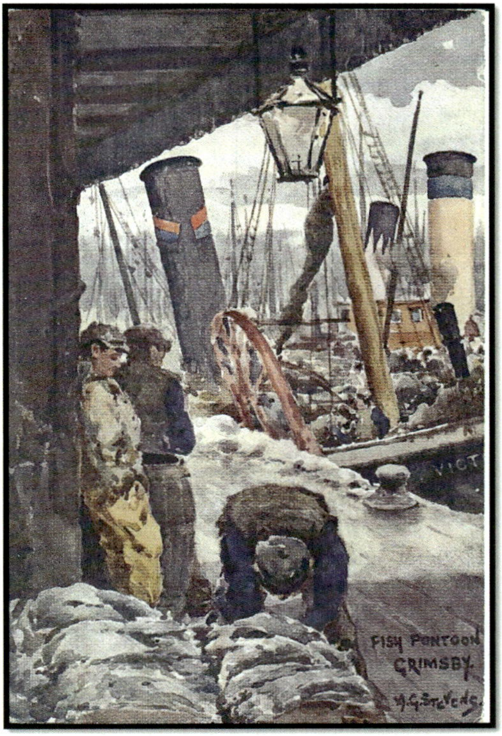

Fish Pontoon Grimsby. A G Stevens

In this painting A G Stevens has captured the extent of the steam trawler fleet based in Grimsby. It was these very vessels which were responsible for the intensive fishing of the North Sea beds which eventually resulted in the demise of the Staithes inshore fishing fleet. Gradually the Staithes fishermen had to give up their traditional employment and in many cases find work in the Cleveland iron stone mines. A centuries old way of life was transformed within one generation having a serious effect upon the whole community.

Frederic Stuart Richardson 1855-1934

Frederic Richardson was born on the 9th of December, 1855. His father the Rev John Richardson was the rector at Sandy in Bedfordshire and so until his father's death in 1913, Frederic was based at the rectory where he had his studio. This means that Frederic was one of the members of the Staithes Art Club who did not live permanently in the Staithes area but made regular pilgrimages to this scene of so much artistic activity.

However, even though Frederic was based in Bedfordshire, his family had deep roots in the Staithes area. His grandfather was a chemist in Whitby and his great grandfather was a ship's chandler in Staithes itself at a time when the village had a considerable fleet of fishing vessels.

Richardson received a fortunate legacy in 1877 which changed his life for he was now able to stop his training as an engineer and dedicate all his time and energy to his one love, painting. Being aware of the revolutionary artistic movements on the continent, Richardson went to Paris to receive tuition from the Academic Painter Carolus Duran 1837-1917. (Carolus Duran was the head of one of the principal *ateliers* in Paris. He taught some of the greatest artists of the next generation including John Singer Sargent and so Frederic Richardson had chosen the best that Paris could offer.)

While in Paris, Richardson met other artists who would eventually form the Staithes Group of Artists and so he always tried to visit Staithes whenever possible. Things were made even easier for Frederic to visit Staithes when his brother who lived at Park Hall, Aislaby near to Whitby, offered Frederic facilities to continue his painting in the Whitby area. In 1902 Frederic was elected as a full member of the Staithes Art Club.

Frederic Richardson also had links with the artistic activity in Cornwall and it was while there he met Elsie Reynolds whom he married and they honeymooned in Holland. He was a frequent traveller and with other members of the Staithes group, visited Fred and Hannah Mayor at Montreuil-sur-Mer.

Richardson received much acclaim during his lifetime and was elected a member of most of the prestigious Art Societies. He exhibited in Glasgow, Liverpool, Manchester, and Birmingham but this part of his life is outside of what could be called his 'Staithes period'. In 1917 he had moved to Ashton near Bristol and he remained there until his death on the 22nd of April, 1934 when he was aged 78.

The diversity and quality of the work he left behind will always be a tribute to one of the most able of the Staithes Group of Artists.

Percy Morton Teasdale 1870-1961

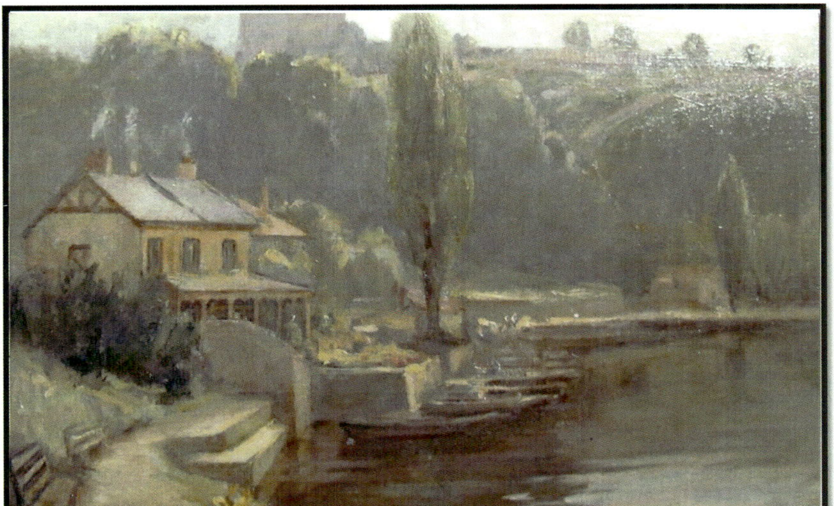

The Nidd below Knaresborough Castle.

Courtesy of the Pannett Art Gallery, Whitby

Percy Morton Teasdale like Henry Rowland Hill studied painting under Sir Hubert von Herkomer at his school in Bushey in Hertfordshire. Like so many members of the Staithes Group, he travelled to Paris to continue his studies at the Académie Julian. To supplement his income from sales of paintings he taught at the Harrogate School of Art and also the Leeds School of Art. He didn't become a member of the Staithes Art Club until 1905. He was particularly fond of painting in the picturesque regions of the West Riding as indicated in this view of Knaresborough.

James Watson 1851-1936

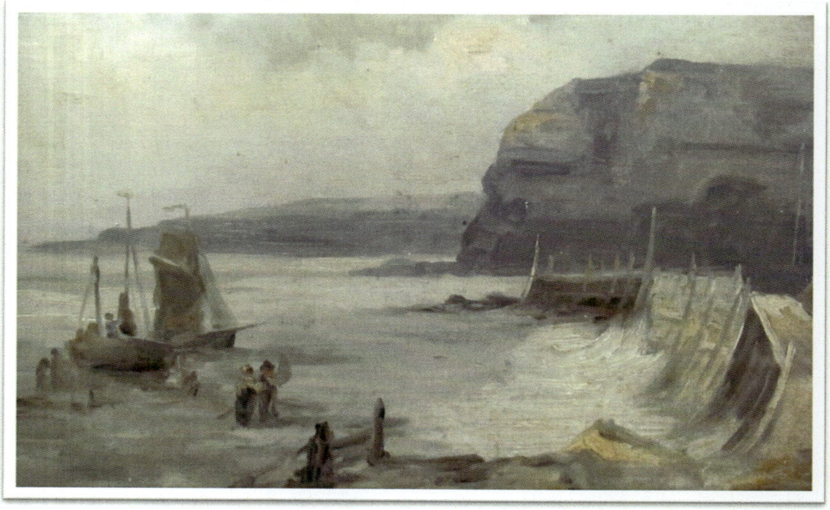

Courtesy of the Pannett Art Gallery, Whitby

A characteristic of the Staithes Group of Artists was the degree of commitment from the various members. Some had decided to settle in the Staithes area and were fully committed to work among their colleagues and experience the pressures of making a living from their paintings. Others visited only during the summer months or when their regular employment gave them a window of opportunity to join in with the group.

James Watson was from the second category. He was art master at Newcastle Royal Grammar School from 1876 to 1919 which coincided with the whole of the period of the Staithes Group. It was not until 1919 when he ceased teaching that he was able to live in a cottage in Brown's Terrace, Hinderwell. He remained there until 1930.

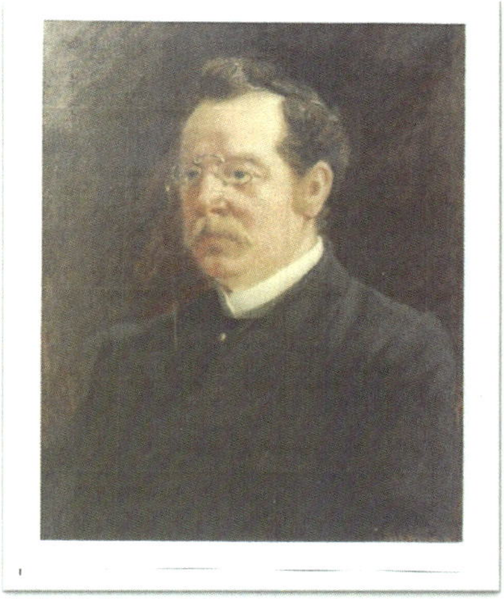

Painting of James Watson by J.W.Gilroy and dated (19)01

The Newcastle Journal for the 27th of March 1936 contained such a detailed tribute to James Watson that I have quoted it here in full.

MR. JAMES WATSON

Former Art Master at City Grammar School

The death is announced at the advanced age of 84 of Mr James Watson, at 23. Beverley Gardens, Cullercoates. He was for 43 years art master at the Newcastle Grammar School. A native of Newcastle, he was educated at the old Heber Tower School, and received his art training at the South Kensington School of Art, London. He was appointed to Newcastle Grammar School in 1876 and retired in 1919. He took art classes in connexion with the Newcastle Municipal Evening School scheme of former years and also conducted night art classes at South Shields. For some years he was art inspector to Durham County Education authorities.

He was vice-president of the Bewick Club and exhibited in the Royal Academy. Formerly an ardent bowler, he was an old Summerhill man, and at one time he was an active member of the St. John's Lodge of Freemasons, Newcastle. After his retirement he went to reside at Hinderwell, Yorkshire, but upon the death of his wife six years ago, he went to reside with a member of his family at Cullercoates. He is survived by three sons and a daughter. The funeral is to take place at Hinderwell to-morrow.

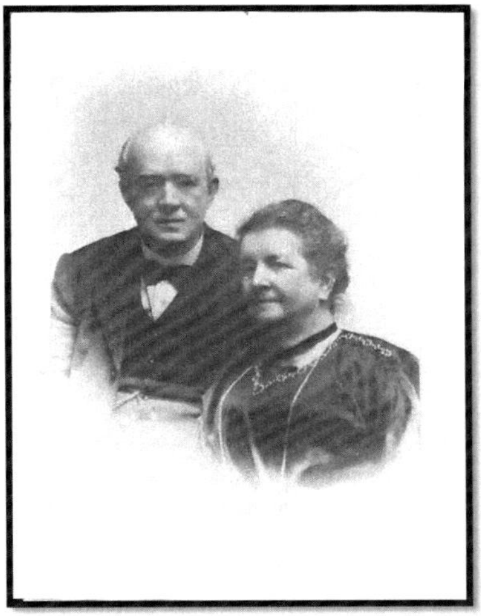

A later photograph of James Watson with his wife Isabella

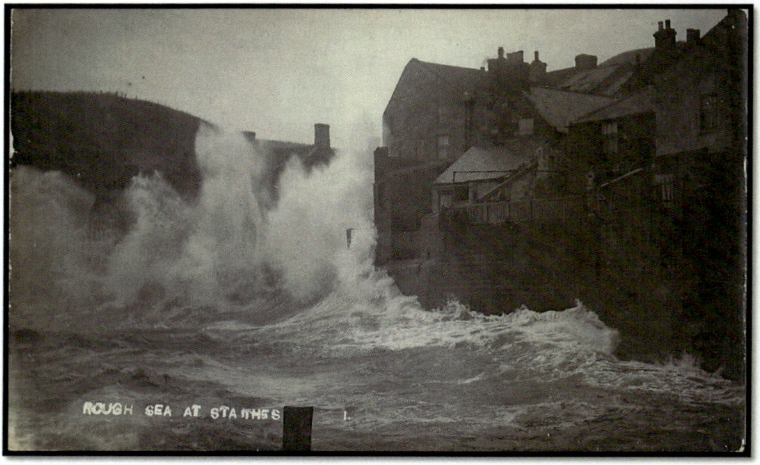

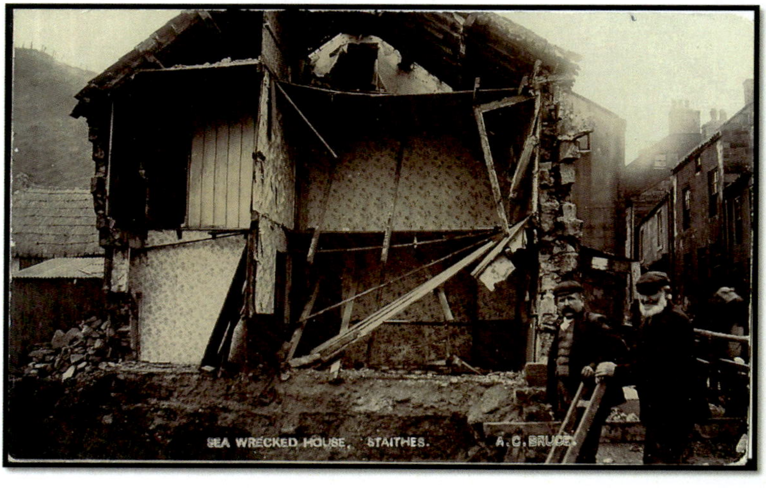

The power of the North Sea

Part three

Information for further study

The Pannett Art Gallery in Whitby

Beyond doubt the Pannett Art Gallery in Whitby houses the most comprehensive collection of paintings produced by the Staithes Group in the whole of the United Kingdom.

The core of the permanent exhibition was formed by George Bednar who carefully sought examples of as many different members of the group as possible. These are now in Whitby as a tribute to the work of artists who captured everyday life in this isolated region of North Yorkshire over a century ago.

A special room was set aside in the Pannett Gallery in May 1995 to house George Bednar's acquisitions of oil paintings and watercolours which were mainly produced in the golden years of 1894 to 1909 although he also included works in some cases which had been created in later life after the group had dispersed.

So important are the works in the Pannett collection that occasionally paintings have been sent out on loan to other national galleries to augment their temporary exhibitions. An example is the large watercolour '*Staithes Fisherman*' by Laura Johnson (Knight) which was shown recently at Penlee House Penzance, Djanogly Art Gallery Nottingham and Worcester Art Gallery. .

A feature of the Pannett collection is that paintings are not centred on one specific artist but include examples from most of the members of the group. Also the collection includes various genres. Mark Senior's oil painting '*A Market in Bruges*' and Rowland Hill's oil painting '*Continental Street Scene*' reminds one of the close links between individual members of the Staithes Group and colonies of artists on the continent. Owen Bowen's '*Roses in a Vase*', Hannah Mayor's '*Roses in a Vase*' and Edward Conway's still life with flowers demonstrate that not all the work was produced *en plein air* and the two engravings by John Wright are an indication of the graphic work produced by both Frank Mason and Laura Knight during the early 1920's. By far the main emphasis is on the cobles, the fishing nets, crab pots and the toil of the fisher wives as they carry to their husband's boat the baited long lines on skeps on their heads. In fact the whole panorama of life in this small fishing community has been captured by these artists.

In 1904 the first exhibition of work of the Staithes Group to be held in Whitby was at Anderson's Gallery in Skinner Street only a short distance from the Pannett Gallery. The opening of the Staithes Room in the Pannett Gallery in 1995 over ninety years later was an apt confirmation of the lasting quality of the work produced by these early pioneers of 'Modern British Art'.

On the following pages I have listed a catalogue of the contents of the Staithes Room. Like Mussorgsky in his '*Pictures from an Exhibition*' I also have promenaded round the room in a clockwise direction looking at each painting in turn. The titles given to the paintings are not those of the original artist but given here to help identify the work.

The Pannett Collection

1 Charles Hodge Mackie 1862-1920 Watercolour
Whitby Harbour 1900

2 Rowland Henry Hill 1873-1952 Watercolour
Falkingbridge Wine Merchamts

3 Joseph Alfred Terry 1872-1939 Oil
Italian moonlight scene

4 Frederick William Jackson 1859-1918 Oil
The Pool of London

5 Henry Silkstone Hopwood 1860-1914 Watercolour
A Whitby Jet Worker

6 Robert Jobling 1841 – 1923 Watercolour
A *Street in Staithes*

7 Hirst Walker 1868 – 1957 Watercolour
The Five Monks Whitby

8 Henry Silkstone Hopwood 1860- 1914 Watercolour
A Whitby Jet Worker

9 Albert George Stevens 1863-1925 Watercolour
A Jet Turner

10 Laura Johnson (Knight) 1877-1970 Watercolour
Staithes Quay

11 Thomas Barrett 1845-1924 Aquatint
Gathering Flithers

12 Hannah Mayor 1871-1947 Watercolour
Fisherman and coble

13 Laura Knight 1877-1970 Watercolour
Grace

14 Andrew Charles Colley 1859-1910 Oil
No title – man in front of stove

15 Leandro Garsido 1868-1909 Oil
The Scullery Maid

16 Ernest Higgins Rigg 1868-1947 Oil
A Fireside Read

17 Frederick Stuart Richardson 1855-1934 Watercolour
Whitby Bridge from the Fish Quay

18 Joseph Richard Bagshawe 1870-1909 Watercolour
The Staithes Yawl 'Truelove'

19 Arthur James Wetherall Burgess 1879-1957 Watercolour
Catching the breeze

20 Ernest Dade 1864-1935 Watercolour
Herring Cobles going to sea

21 Lionel Townsend Crawshaw 1864-1949 Oil
Whitby Old Bridge

22 James Watson 1851-1936 Oil
Port Mulgrave

23 Lionel Townsend Crawshaw Oil
Hauling Cobles, Runswick Bay

24 Hon. Duff Tollemache 1859-1936 Oil
No title- Sailing boat and dinghy

25 William Gilbert Foster 1855-1906 Oil
Cabbage patch at Runswick

26 Rowland Henry Hill 1873-1952 Watercolour
Flowergate Whitby

27 Robert Jobling 1841-1923 Watercolour
Moonlight over Whitby

28 Laura Johnson (Knight) 1877-1970 Watercolour
Staithes Fisherman

29 Florence Hess 1891-1974 Oil
No title-family on beach

30 Harrington Mann 1864-1937 Oil
Low Tide on the Beach

31 John Bowman 1872? -1915 Oil
Ugthorpe Mill, 1907

32 William Gilbert Foster 1855-1906 Oil
Cottages at Runswick Bay

33 Robert Jobling 1841-1923 Oil
Staithes

34 Harold Knight 1874-1961 Oil
Leaving Harbour, Evening

35 Arthur Friedenson 1872-1955 Oil
The calm after the storm. 1897

36 Joseph Richard Bagshawe 1870-1909 Watercolour
Cobles leaving Staithes

37 Frank Henry Mason 1876-1965 Watercolour
Whitby Herring Cobles

38 William Frederick Mayor 1866-1916 Watercolour
Snow at Hinderwell

39 Frank Henry Mason 1876-1965 Oil
Whitby in the days of Oak and Hemp

40 Frederick Stuart Richardson 1855-1934 Watercolour
Stormy weather Staithes

41 Laura Johnson (Knight) 1877-1970 Watercolour
New Quay Road Whitby

42 Rowland Henry Hill 1873-1952 Oil
Continental Street Scene

43 Edward (Harold Edgar) Conway 1872-1949
No title – (Vase of flowers)

44 Percy Morton Teasdale 1870-1961 Oil
The Nidd below Knaresborough .
Castle

45 Owen Bowen 1873-1967 Oil
Hawsker Mill

46 John Wright 1857-1933 Watercolour
A Yorkshire Gorge

47 John Atkinson 1863-1924 Oil
Egton Horse Fair

48 John Wright 1857-1933 Etching
The Canal at Sluis Holland

49 Albert George Stevens 1863-1925 Watercolour
Cattle in a barn

50 Isa Jobling 1851-1926 Pen and ink
The Goose Girl

51 Hannah Mayor 1871-1947 Oil
A Spring Bouquet

52 Owen Bowen 1873-1967 Oil
Roses in a vase

53 John Atkinson 1863-1924 Oil
Harvesting, North Yorkshire

54 James William Booth 1867-1953 Oil
In the stables

55 James Watson 1851-1936 Watercolour
Sandsend

56 Sidney Valentine Gardener d1957 Oil
View from the river bank

57 Charles Cutts Elmshirst 1872-1937 Oil
A Humber Kneel under Sail

58 Frederick William Jackson 1859-1918 Oil
The Last Load

59 John Wright 1857-1933 Engraving
The Italian Girl

60 Paul Paul 1865-1937 Oil
A Shepherd and his Flock

61 Isa Jobling 1851-1926 Oil
Girl in a Cottage Garden

62 Ralph Hedley 1848-1913 Oil
The Reaper

63 John Bowman 1872? -1915 Oil
No title – open fields

64 Arthur Friedenson 1872-1955 Oil
Stormy Weather, Poole Harbour

Item 29 the oil painting by Florence Hess- Florence Hess was the most junior member of the group as she was only 18 years of age when the group disbanded in 1909. Her main connection with the Staithes Group is that she was taught by Mark Senior who remained in Runswick after the main group had left the area.

The following members of the Staithes Group are not represented in the Pannett Collection -Joseph Alfred Terry 1872-1939, Edward Enoch Anderson 1878-1961.

****

List of the members of the Staithes Group of Artists 1894-1909

The title Staithes Group of Artists is a generic title and includes both members of the Staithes Art Club and the many artists who had a less formal association with the group. In 1901 the Staithes Art Club was established with the election of members with the express purpose of promoting the fellowship, with pooling expertise and, as was the case, the organisation of exhibitions of their work.

1901- THE CREATION OF THE STAITHES ART CLUB

Chairman Henry Silkstone Hopwood 1860-1914
Secretary Joseph Richard Bagshawe 1870-1909
Treasurer Thomas Barrett 1845-1924

1901 MEMBERS

John Bowman 1872 –c1915
Harold Edward Conway 1872-c1923
Ernest (Ernst) Dade 1865-1935
Arthur Friedenson 1872-1955
Hannah Hoyland (Hannah Mayor) 1871-1947
John Spence Ingall 1850-1936
Frederick William Jackson 1859-1918
Robert Jobling 1841-1923
Laura Johnson (Laura Knight) 1877-1970
Harold Knight1874-1961
Charles Hodge Mackie 1862-1920
Frank Mason 1876-1965
William Frederick Mayor 1866-1916
Ernest Higgins Rigg 1868-1947
Mark Senior 1862-1927
Albert George Stevens 1863-1925

1902 MEMBERS

James William Booth 1867-1953
Isa Jobling 1851-1926
Frederic Stuart Richardson 1855-1934

1903 MEMBERS

Sidney V. Gardner d. 1927
James Watson 1851-1936

1904 MEMBERS

Edward Enoch Anderson 1878-1961
Owen Bowen 1873-1967
Lionel Townsend Crawshaw 1864-1949
John Wright 1857-1933

1905 MEMBERS

Paul Paul 1865-1937
Percy Morton Teasdale 1870-1961

1906 MEMBERS

Leandro Ramon Garrido 1868-1909
Joseph Alfred Terry1872-1939

1907 MEMBERS

John Atkinson 1863-1924

Charles Cutts Elmhirst d.1912

NON MEMBERS OF THE STAITHES ART CLUB

Andrew Colley d.1910

Ralph Hedley 1851-1913

Florence Hess 1891-1974

Hirst Walker 1868-1957

The 1909 Diaspora

The title 'The 1909 Diaspora' has two provisos, firstly, some members of the group actually left Staithes before 1909 and secondly, it was only a partial diaspora for there were those members who decided to remain in the Staithes area, for to them the beauty and fascination of the area outweighed the need to move to a more important centre of civilisation to enhance their careers.

There seemed to be various reasons for the golden period of the Staithes Group to eventually terminate. First of all, the Staithes way of life could become oppressive and the regular North Easterly storms with often tragic consequences to the fishing fleet were wearing until eventually things became too overpowering and some members thought there was a need to find a brighter clime, new friends and a fresh chapter to their lives. In this category were Harold and Laura Knight. Harold especially was affected by the 'heaviness' of living in Staithes and so in 1907 they decided to move south and join the community in Newlyn in Cornwall.

For others, such as Fred and Hannah Mayor, family pressure forced their departure as early as 1902 when they fled to Montreuil-sur-Mer though in their hearts they still remained loyal to their many friends in Staithes. Arthur Friedenson, an important and accomplished member of the group had decided to move to Wareham in Dorset in 1908 and this in itself must have been a prime reason for the break up the following year.

On a sombre note, the death of Richard Joseph Bagshawe in 1909 meant that the club was deprived of its treasurer, an energetic supporter of all things and an artist of the highest calibre.

And so after these, as it were 'casualties', the death throes of the Staithes Art Club seemed inevitable.

But some remained, Rowland Henry Hill at Ellerby, Albert George Stevens in Whitby, James Watson in Hinderwell and Mark Senior in Runswick though the original fellowship had ended.

Staithes wasn't entirely forgotten for in the 1940's and 50's there lived in the village an exceptional artist of the next generation, who alone continued the tradition of recording the Staithes way of life and she was Lilian Colbourn 1897-1967.

Almost ironically, in the 1950's her work was shown at the Mayor Gallery in London, the very gallery established by the second son of Fred and Hannah Mayor.

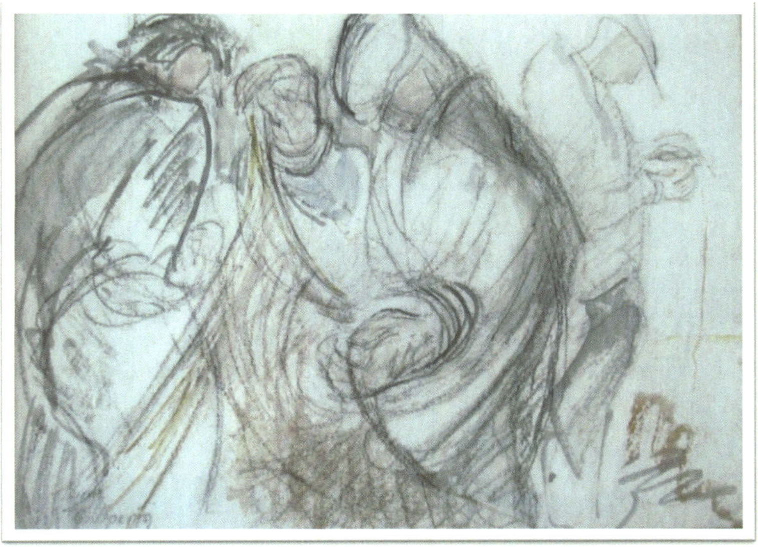

Staithes fishermen. Lilian Colbourn Private collection

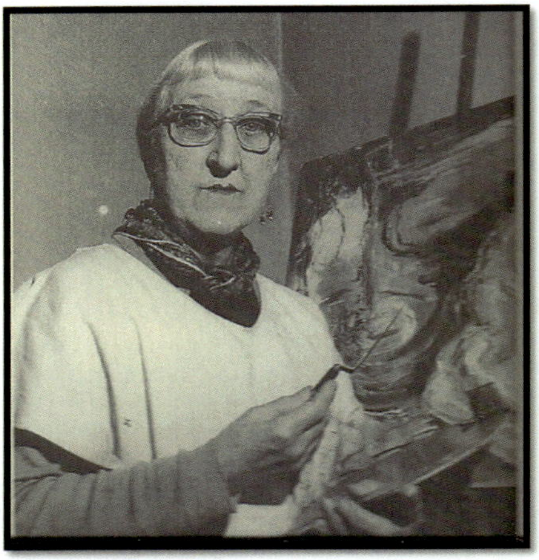

Lilian Colbourn

Bibliography

General reference books

Bullamore,Colin *Scarborough and Whitby Watercolourists*

Published privately 1976

Bullamore,Colin *Ross, Photographer, Whitby*

Published privately 2009

Child,Dennis *The Yorkshire Union of Artists 1888-1922*

Leeds Philosophical and Literary Society 2001

Eccleston, Jean and Peter *A History and Geology of Staithes*

Private Publication 1998

Hart, James (Editor) *The Secret Staithes Diary*

Historical Publishing 2010

Jewell, Rod *Staithes 'Between two nabs'*

Published privately 2013

Haworth, Peter *Paintings by Members of the Staithes Group*

Issued as an exhibition catalogue 2002

Jordan, Rosamund *Staithes Group Centenary Exhibition*

October 2003

Newton, Laura (Editor) *Painting at the edge*

Sansom & Company 2005

Phillips, Peter *The Staithes Group* 1993

Phillips, Peter (Editor) *The Staithes Group of Artists 1894-1909*

Published by the Pannett Gallery Whitby

References to specific artists

Bagshawe, Gerald W. *The Wooden Ships of Whitby*

Horne & Son Whitby 1933

Broadley, Rosie *Laura Knight Portraits*

National Portrait Gallery London 2013

Dade, Ernest *Sail and Oar*

Dent & Son London 1933. Reprinted 2014

Fox, Caroline *Dame Laura Knight*

Phaidon Press Ltd. 1988

Frank, Peter *Sea Painter The Life and work of J.R.Bagshawne*

Phillimore & Co. Ltd. 2010

Knight, Laura *Oil Paint and Grease Paint*

Ivor Nicholson & Watson 1936

Knight, Laura *The Magic of Line*

London 1965

Knowles, Elizabeth *Laura Knight in the Open Air*

Penlee House 2012

Morden, Barbara C. *Laura Knight. A Life*

McNidder & Grace 2014

Acknowledgements

Before I record my gratitude to those who have helped me in preparing this work, I would like to express my thanks to Tom and Rosamund Jordan for their ceaseless effort to ensure that the Staithes artists receive due recognition. Without their years of research and endless exhibitions, the Staithes Group would still be without the acclaim they deserve.

I am grateful to Scarborough Town Council for permission to include illustrations of the paintings in the Pannett Art Gallery in Whitby and to Helen Berry the curator of the gallery.

I would like to thank the librarians of the Whitby Philosophical and Literary Society, to David Taylor, the great grandson of James Watson for family records, to Gloria Wilson daughter of Lilian Colbourn and to Rod Jewell for newly discovered photographs of Gilbert Foster and Frederick Jackson

Finally, my gratitude to my wife Janet for her patience during the time I spent writing this book and for her proof reading and suggestions for improving the text.

Colin Bullamore 2014

Photographs taken during the period of the Staithes Group of Artists

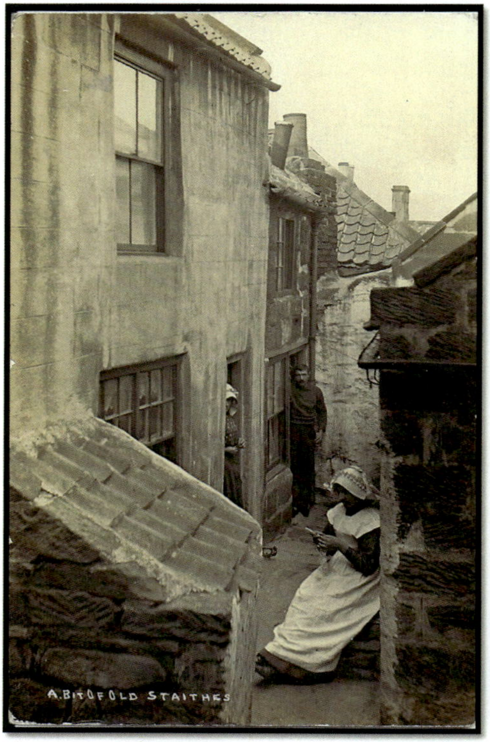

'A bit of old Staithes' by J.T.Ross

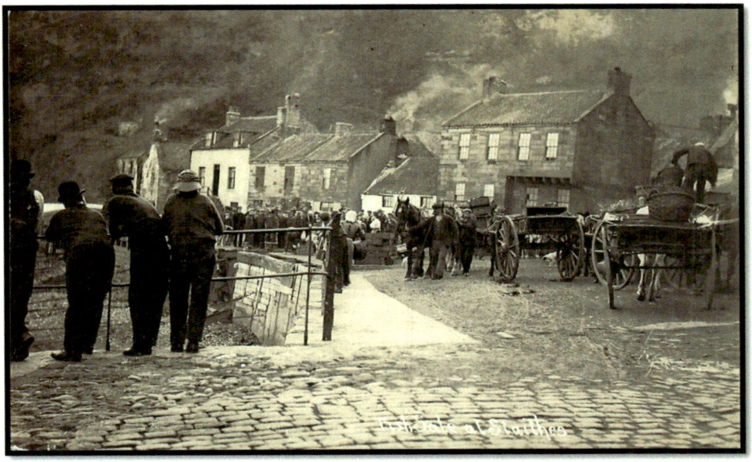

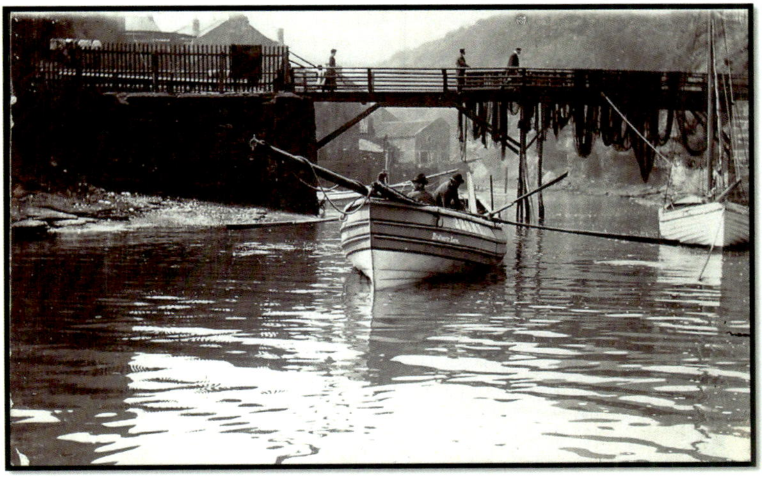

Photographs by H.C.Morley

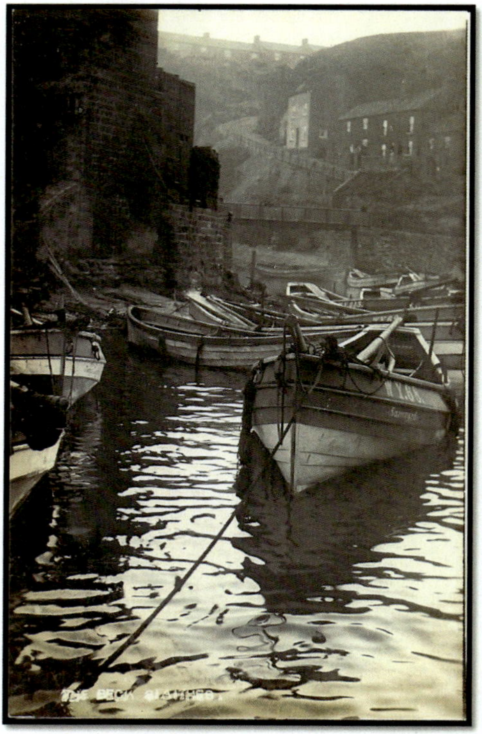
THE BECK